GRANDMOTHERLAND

To the memory of Flo,
my own dear grandmother

Florence Alice Catchpole

*Tho' Dead yet Dear, Tho' Dear yet Dead to me.
Dead is her Body, Dear her Memory*

GRANDMOTHERLAND
Exploring the Myths and the Realities

Judith Edwards

KARNAC
firing the mind

First published in 2024 by
Karnac Books Limited
62 Bucknell Road
Bicester
Oxfordshire OX26 2DS

British Library Cataloguing in Publication Data

A C.I.P. for this book is available from the British Library

ISBN-13: 978-1-913494-77-3

Typeset by vPrompt eServices Pvt Ltd, India

Printed in the United Kingdom

www.firingthemind.com

To Sam and his children

Contents

Acknowledgements

I am very grateful to my publishers, Christina Wipf Perry and Kate Pearce, and their colleagues at Confer and Karnac respectively, and to Professor Brett Kahr for his encouragement from the beginning—and then to all the wise and wonderful people, mainly women, from various cultural backgrounds and ethnicities, who have contributed to this book, both by talking and by writing their own accounts, at my request. Most of them have chosen to remain anonymous, though I have given them pseudonymous first names where appropriate You know who you are, and you have my heartfelt gratitude. These accounts are the backbone of the book, and many of the contributors did not really know what they would write till they started writing, as they said. Lastly, but certainly not least, my husband, Andrew Baldwin, who has supported me unfailingly with anything to which I have turned my hand.

About the author

Judith Edwards is a child and adolescent psychotherapist who has worked for over thirty years at the Tavistock Clinic in London. *Love the Wild Swan: The Selected Works of Judith Edwards* was published by Routledge in their World Library of Mental Health series, and her edited book, *Psychoanalysis and Other Matters: Where Are We Now?* was also published by Routledge. From 1996 to 2000, she was joint editor of the *Journal of Child Psychotherapy*. Apart from her clinical experience, one of her principal interests is in the links between psychoanalysis, culture, and the arts, as well as making psychoanalytic ideas accessible to a wider audience. She has an international academic publishing record and in 2010 was awarded the Jan Lee memorial prize for the best paper linking psychoanalysis and the arts during that year: 'Teaching and learning about psychoanalysis Film as a teaching tool'.

Preface

There are many books now available on Amazon and in bookshops about how to be a grandparent. Books with titles like *The Complete Guide to Becoming a Grandmother* or *Grandparenting: A Survival Guide*. Is this because we've lost the knack, because it's become more tricky, or just because books are now easier to write and publish? Or do people want to get to the end of the story before scrolling through all the events that led up to it?

This book is certainly not a 'how to' book. I would ask that you simply look at the chapters here and see which one grabs you first, then just motor on, browsing as you please.

'A book must be the axe that smashes the frozen sea within us,' suggested the early twentieth-century writer and philosopher Franz Kafka (1883–1924, letter to Oskar Pollak dated 27 January 1904). We should read, he said, for more than simply mere entertainment, we should consider reading because the world is more than the things that happen in the world. There is too much crystallisation within us—products of everyday life and defence mechanisms we employ to turn away from life—which can only be broken by the axe of intimate and profound reading. So hopefully this book may smash a few preconceptions and give us a more nuanced view of 'the way things are', so we may receive what Kafka called 'a blow to the head'. We need, he said, books that 'affect us like a disaster' and this eventually leads to freedom.

I will, with my thirty-five years of experience working with families from different cultures, take you for a ride through Grandmotherland, exploring the accepted 'norms'. I'll be looking at the reason why naming your emotions can help prevent them from draining you. It may be better to have 'small' rather than 'great' expectations. It's worth noting how much the accident of our birthplace can separate us from sets of opinions held elsewhere about grandmothers.

I hope to offer a few ideas about what may lie underneath these sets of opinion held in the Western world. What is 'the norm'? Who decides what name will be chosen for grandmothers? Gran or Grannie or Grandma, Nan or Nana? One story in the book tells of a grandmother who wished to be called 'Persephone'—though she allowed her grandchildren to change it later. And one of my patients was called G by her grandchildren. Is this a way of avoiding ageing? Rather than being prescriptive, I think one has to explore each title, each time, with each person and each family. Sets of opinions may prevail indeed, and what lies underneath these 'opinions'? 'Set' may be the word: do we have set ideas which are beyond changing? Can we revise these, or do they remain stuck as constant and unchangeable views? As the Persian mystic and poet Rumi averred in the thirteenth century, conventional opinion is the ruin of our souls. When does history turn to myth and myth back into history?

I hope readers may find something I too didn't know before I wrote the book, but I can expect this only from those readers who perhaps expect to read something *they* did not previously know. New ideas may spring up inside us all. It has been a joy and a privilege for me to write this book: I hope my readers may also find some satisfaction here. Will you be the same self you were before? This does not aim to be 'the last word' on the subject of grandparenting, and of grandmothers in particular, whether she is called Gran or Grannie, Grandma, Nan or Nana. There are of course class implications which are beyond my remit here. I am limiting myself to a few of the more salient and prominent issues, as if I were working with scissors and miles of film footage. My thoughts are edited, as are everybody's. Join the conversation, follow the path and see where it takes you.

The interviews happened during the time of Covid, so were all online, and comprised people from both my personal and my professional background, taken from roughly a dozen responses.

As I have emphasised, this is not a 'how to' book—my clinical experience has shown me that we need to take our time and to take each 'case' in an individual way. There are no blanket prescriptions, indeed these are to be avoided, as one could miss the subtle nuances of each individual's presentation of themselves to the world. I hope to avoid omniscience, psychoanalytic or otherwise, and leave each reader to have their own thoughts, which may change, or may not, according to what she or he reads. This is how the best work is done and the best lives are led.

In which we begin the journey and see where we go

Granny takes a trip, leaving the empty rocking chair without being 'off her rocker'

Okay, we get in the car, we fasten our seatbelts, we switch on the ignition (or maybe press the button on an electrically powered twenty-first-century car), we've checked the tyres and the oil and the water, the engine fires and off we go on our exploration. We have a map (a sat nav would be far too prescriptive, we may do a fair bit of slow meandering) but our ultimate destination is a mystery. All journeys have secret destinations, of which the traveller may be unaware. This is what I have discovered in my clinical work over many years. Lots of note taking. How does a book take its shape? Do all our lives go backwards, like a rewound film, to our beginnings? While we think we are going forwards, do our individual journeys take us in the other direction on a trip within? I started writing this book with thoughts of my own grandmother (see frontispiece) and that experience then took me forward to my experience now and the experiences of many other people I have contacted. An atlas of emotions can be very helpful and my contributors have all provided pages to this atlas.

Grandparents are the parents of a person's father or mother—paternal or maternal. Every sexually reproducing living organism has a maximum of four genetic grandparents, eight genetic great-grandparents, sixteen genetic great-great-grandparents, thirty-two genetic great-great-great-grandparents. Our DNA takes us onwards, ever onwards. Do the maths. In the history of modern humanity, around seventy thousand years ago, the number of human beings who lived to be grandparents increased. We don't know for certain what spurred this increase in long lives—the results may largely be to do with improved medical technology and living standards—but it's generally believed that a key consequence of three generations being alive together would be the preservation of information which could otherwise be lost. More on this anon.

Grandparents are second-degree relatives of their grandchildren, as I have said, and share a twenty-five per cent genetic overlap. What do grannies offer? In cases where parents are unwilling or unable to provide adequate care for their children (e.g. financial obstacles, marriage problems, illness or death), grandparents often take on the role of primary caregivers. Even when this is not the case, and particularly in traditional cultures (see Chapter 3), grandparents often have a direct and clear role in relation to the raising, care, and nurture of children.

Looking at the 'normal' expectations of a grandmother, who has a genetic connection with her grandchildren, altruism tops the list. The most defining characteristic of effective grandparents is seen to be their altruistic orientation towards life. Altruism, an interesting word, but maybe a little exploration would be good here. It's derived from the Latin 'alter' (meaning other) and the French 'autrui' (meaning other person's). So, it's defined as unselfish devotion to the needs of others. It is quite the opposite of egoism or self-centredness. Yet there is another view: are any altruistic acts devoid of ego and sense of self? Don't we all feel good about ourselves when we do things for others? I suspect the answer is invariably yes …

Every granny has desires about being a good granny and wants them to come true. Desires are at the heart of stories. It is almost unknown for the realisation of wishes and goals to follow a certain pattern. However, true desires and goals arise in you and fulfil you, they enrich your life in every way. Non-true wishes and goals, meanwhile, come from outside—someone else is calling the tune, they can have dangerous, even destructive, effects and are not conducive to your development. The advertising industry and social media come to mind. Like any superpower, desires can be used for 'good' or for 'ill'. These desires result in narrative fractures, and there can be an ongoing battle over whose story we adhere to. Does desire suggest lack? If I want this but can't have it, can you be allowed to have it too? 'I'm going to impose *my* fantasy on you.' A mindset is simply a collection of beliefs that shape our habits and actions: thoughts become beliefs, beliefs become 'how things ought to be'. This might be thought of as 'normal'. But whose normal?

If we accept, as many people now do, that 'being a mother' is perhaps a painted scene behind which the reality is much more varied (and maybe more interesting), will this exploration into the role of grannies help us all be free of preconceptions, change or lower our expectations, and live the life we've got rather than the one we're led to expect? I recall many years ago a mother saying very honestly to me, 'Ah yes, there's the Mothercare baby, then there's the one you get, which can be very different.' She was able to accept that her fantasies had been only fantasies and that the reality she experienced was somewhat at odds with these. If we have this yearning to be the same as other people in a rush of mimetic desire—I want to be just like her because she seems to 'have it all'—can we tolerate and accept difference rather than feeling we have 'failed' some given norm? As one of my anonymous correspondents said, 'I am always startled by people who have no memory of their grandparents. For me, they have helped make me me, they are as much a part of my identity as my arms and legs.' That's one view, grandparents seen almost as anatomical parts, but are we able to look at things up close in individual cases rather than seeing larger patterns as repeated in small lives and then seen as what we might term self-evident, both in this book and in a wider sense? As I have emphasised, each 'case' will have its own set of rules and one small change can alter the pattern.

So what is the white Western received wisdom about being a good-enough grandmother? How should we play the part? Should we be a character rather than a caricature? Rule number one seems to be to offer to babysit. If you're not up for it because disabilities prevent you from taking on the task, that's already a strike against you. Of course, if you work and don't have the time, that's another strike. You should offer to help around the house and never, ever talk about how the baby resembles your side of the family, unless you are specifically asked to comment. Don't talk about the baby loving you, and tell mum she's doing a great job. (I recall an observer who became upset when the baby's aunt tried to get the baby to call her 'Mamma' when Mamma was out of the room. It was a covert tussle for ownership, and was of course confusing for the baby.) When you're out shopping, call and ask if the child's mother needs anything. Don't show anyone the pictures you may get sent of the grandchild. Oh, that *is* hard!

We all come to grandparenting with different expectations, different internal stories, often derived from our own grandparents (see Chapter 7). Some grandparents want to be involved in every aspect of their grandchildren's lives. They post the ultrasounds of the little germinating soul on social media. As this poem by one of my contributors indicates, some grandparents are there for every internal development:

> Hello Hello
> You're there I know
> Each day I see your Mother grow
> Heavier
> More beautiful and slow.
>
> Deep, deep
> You sleep
> And stretch and swim
> In secret waters warm
> Where archetypal dreams arise
> And float before your unborn eyes
> And feet and fingers form.
>
> To you in there
> So close, so far
> The dead are no more distant
> Than the living are.
> You are a part of them
> And us.
>
> Red hair perhaps
> Grey eyes?
> An upturned nose?
> A tendency to giggle?
> Your Grandpa's toes?

You are a mixture and a mystery
Unique, brand new and ancient history.
Wisely you bide your time
You wait and grow
I know you're there
Hello Hello.

Some grandparents wish to be present at the birth of this 'mixture and mystery'. Hello hello! They want a front row seat for everything that happens then and subsequently. Some sons and daughters and in-laws are fine with this. And some are not.

Other grandparents are more distant, even hands-off, in their approach. They don't want day-to-day reports about sleeping and poo-ing and teething and rolling over. They've done that once and are not interested in repeating the experience. They don't want to make video calls every night. And they certainly don't want to babysit. Some sons and daughters and in-laws are fine with this, too. But not all of them.

It's when the grandparents want one thing and the parents want another that there's trouble in the garden. Then everything in the garden will not be lovely, at all. As one correspondent said, 'Honestly, we all try to do our blooming best but can still be thwarted, as every situation has a different chemistry.' Indeed.

But here's the vital thing to remember about grandparenting: it is not a one-size-fits all, a Grandmother Brand. You can't just pick one off the shelf. Many sons and daughters and in-laws fiercely disagree with their mothers and mothers-in-law. These relationships are custom made every time, in every family, with every individual. What works for one family may well not work for another. The one thing that all grandparents need to remember, whether they are intimately or only occasionally involved in their grandchildren's lives, is that the grand-children are not theirs. They are the children's kids. They don't belong to the grandparents, except by extension.

Which means grandparents don't get to make the rules. None of them. They don't get to decide what time their grandkids go to bed. What they eat and how they eat it. How they address the adults in their lives. What they wear, the length of their hair, or whether or not they should get their ears pierced. Or get a tattoo.

Their parents make all these decisions. Unless we are raising our grandchildren, unless we are their official caretakers, we are categorically not in charge. We've had our turn. We ruled the roost with our own children. Now our children get to rule the roost with theirs. It's that simple. Except, of course, it isn't, don't they know that? Because we know things. Because we've been down this road and we have insights and experiences we want to share with our children to make things easier for them. We might want to say, 'It's easier if the kids go to bed early, if their clothes are chosen for them, if they sit and eat breakfast and not run around all over the place.'

As one of my anonymous correspondents said,

> For many years, my tongue was nearly raw from biting it so much, from saying nothing to my grown-up, full-fledged adult children who clearly were not raising their children the way I would raise them. *Why are you giving him sweets when you told him nine times already that he couldn't have any? What do you mean, she dresses herself? She can't go out looking like that! What a fright! He's knows enough words to tell you exactly how you should wipe his bum. Don't you think he's ready to be toilet-trained?* I said none of these things. But I wanted to.

Now, after twelve years of grandparenting, she said, her tongue is never sore. Why? Because she doesn't bite it any more. Because she (finally!) understands what her role is. It's absolutely not on to say, 'Do it my way. My way is the right way.' It's not her place to offer advice, unless she is asked directly. And she mustn't walk around with disapproval on her face. 'My kids must raise their kids the way they choose,' she admits. This is the mindset she has finally achieved. Even unvoiced disapproval can be felt, by the adults and by their children too.

She continues the story.

> My old aunt used to say, 'Look at all the adults in the world. Are any of them still sucking dummies?' It was her way of saying, 'Hey, life changes, they'll be okay. Children eventually give up their dummies. They stop jumping around on the furniture. They learn how to chew with their mouths closed and say please and thank you without being reminded.'

Is it bad to have expectations for family relationships? It is if you expect to be in charge. This is the news: you're not! But if you can go with the flow, as the saying goes, if you can trust that your kids are doing the best they can, if your expectations are small, simply to be part of your children's and grandchildren's lives, you can find joy even in what can seem to you like chaos.

So what we can cull from this is that there are ways to be good, to survive, to transit from being a parent to being a grandparent (particularly a grandmother), to doing this 'practically perfectly'. Mmm. Do some myths need revisiting here? Can we learn some new lessons and abandon some preconceptions? Can we venture 'outside the norm', treating it with respectful disregard, and find some different ways of developing a positive spiral?

The slew of books on grandparenting exists in a crowded market. They all subscribe to the myth of being 'good' or 'perfect'. What about those grandparents who don't read these books (though I am sure they make very edifying reading) and instead rely on their own instincts and still somehow get it wrong? Is there a myth that needs to be looked at, beyond the conventional rosy picture: is it cultural, is it familial, is it personal? Grandchildren give their grandparents an assurance of the continuation of life beyond their own death … but does how books are read rely on history or geography? Where you live and how your own history played out? Two sets of feelings about the same 'facts' may be felt as 'madness' if they do not agree with previously accepted norms and are accordingly disliked, but often some unpicking and disentangling can offer a way forward. Thoughts can happily fly around without any one person being responsible for them. These thoughts may seem to exist without a thinker, but they then get corralled into particular narrative tropes. We may be unconscious of how these develop, and over time they can begin to rule the lives of those who espouse them. Dropping our desires is not a bad way forward.

There are of course conscious factors, but we leave out the unconscious at our peril, or so I believe after many years of working with families. As Marilyn Monroe said in a *Guardian* interview in 1962, 'You're always running into people's unconscious.'

Maybe we need to open some doors here, to let in some new air. This may provide some relief. This book may answer no questions but pose even more: as the great psychoanalyst Wilfred Bion said, it is important to keep our questions in good repair. There may be many repetitions of the word 'but' in this cloud of unknowing. When does a fantasy become a myth, and has that myth wrapped within it a core, a kernel, a grain of 'truth'? The first sentence of Tolstoy's *Anna Karenina* is 'Happy families are all alike; every unhappy family is unhappy in its own way'. Well yes, indeed, financial security, good health, good relationships— these are the conscious rational factors which make all happy families alike, whether nuclear or extended. But deeper down, I suggest, there may be other streams at work. An apprehension of unhappiness may exist deep down in all families. What is common to unhappy families, however constituted, is precisely that: unhappiness *is* the stream, with its many tributaries, which run down rivers of grief into the sea of sorrow. So what do grannies believe? What do they want? What do they need to do in order to have a reasonable, even happy, relationship with their grandchildren? Can we revisit and revise the meme, attempting (not always successfully) to empty it out of preconceptions and replace it with other ideas?

Here are some thoughts from the grandchildren themselves.

> A grandmother is a remarkable woman. She's a wonderful combination of warmth and kindness, laughter and love. She overlooks our faults, encourages our dreams, and praises our every success. A grandmother has the wisdom of a teacher, the sincerity of a true friend, and the tenderness of a mother. She's someone we admire, respect and love very much.

> A grandmother is a lady who has no children of her own, so she likes other people's little boys and girls. [*Well she did have children of course, but way back beyond the child's time, which is perhaps too far for the young mind to stretch.*]

> Grandmas don't have to do anything except be there. They're old, so they shouldn't play hard or run. It is enough if they drive us to the market where the pretend horse is and have lots of little money ready. Usually grandmas are fat, but not too fat to tie kids' shoes. They wear glasses and they can take their teeth out and gums off! They don't have to be smart, only answer questions like why dogs chase cats and how come God isn't married? They don't talk Baby Talk like visitors do because it is hard to

understand, and, when they read to us, they don't skip words or mind if it is the same story over and over again. Everyone should try to have a Grandma, especially if they don't have a television, because grandmothers are the only grown-ups who really ever seem to have any time for children!

So there is the idealised version of 'being a grandmother' writ large by the kids who have had the experience. She's old, she's fat, she may be toothless, gum-less (?) but she has *time* for the grandkids. This is the 'you' you should aspire to be.

Then there are the perennially pervasive and largely male 'mother-in-law 'jokes', not at all 'funny' to anyone except the men involved. The mother-in-law, of course, is also the grandmother. But how do we make sense of this split? This book aims to look at the contradictions rather than be 'comfortably numb' to the paradoxes deeply rooted in our way of life and our thinking.

With apologies for the mixed metaphors here, I want to enter the multidimensional web of roads and explore the paradoxes which lie at the heart of this idea of 'being a grandmother'. Is this about 'being' or 'doing'? Do we turn left or right here? Or keep straight on? Turning left or right may not be what the roadmap recommends, but we may find out something about new areas, previously unexplored. We'll be going slowly. How far do we travel outwards in the 'specifically experienced environment'? How much influence does that have? I will not only look at the conventional and largely white Western ideas about 'the good grandmother' but also visit cultures around the world to find out how this meme is seen in various culturescapes. New understandings of the culturescapes often give us new inner-standings. By the way, eating with your hands is absolutely fine in some cultures, in Africa, India, and the Middle East. The collective thought forms gather weight and it's important to think about who is controlling the narrative.

We orient ourselves within a narrative in order to have an idea of who we are. However, narrative 'coherence' can be a trap in itself, as coherence gathers round a point of view which may be only one among many assigned to the topic. Whose 'coherence'? Knowledge of anyone else has to be partly invention: the person at the heart of the 'invention' is constructed as well as invented. David Kessler (2019), who worked with Elisabeth Kübler-Ross on *Death and Dying*, has an instructive way to think about narrative. He advises that we take three facts, two bad, one better. Then think of three bad outcomes from all three, good and bad. Then think of three good outcomes from all three, including the 'bad' ones. Different narratives will be formed, although the facts remain the same. So 'narrative coherence' can depend on point of view. I hope this will be an unsensational but nevertheless interesting account of personal and social phenomena around 'being a granny'.

As parents, those of us who have reproduced ourselves ('Look what I've made,' we may proudly proclaim) have heard about the importance of positive parent–child relationships in the social and emotional development of children. There are countless research studies and supporting statistics (look them up if you wish) that highlight the many benefits that come from strong parent–child bonds. What isn't always recognised, however, is the positive impact that a close relationship between a grandparent and grandchild can have on the happiness and wellbeing of the entire family. Simply put, having grandparents around is good for everyone. A healthy connection between a grandchild and grandparent is beneficial to both sides of the relationship. Grandparents truly impact their grandchildren's lives.

A vast number of adult grandchildren feel that their grandparents influenced their beliefs and values (see Chapter 7). A child's perspective of what constitutes a healthy, normal relationship is shaped by the relationship that they hold with a grandparent. Through regular contact, a sense of emotional intimacy and unwavering support, children can experience what a true, positive relationship should look like. But research shows that more elderly grannies may feel even older rather than younger if they have sole responsibility for active grandchildren.

A 2014 study at Boston College in the United States found that 'an emotionally close relationship between grandparent and grandchild is associated with fewer symptoms of depression for both generations'. For kids, having grandparents around means having the perfect companions to play with and have fun when parents may be too busy with the physical business of life. Grandparents are some of the best partners when it comes to using creativity and imagination to discover the wonders of life. No room for depression here! And in turn, most grandparents truly love their role. Grandparents Apart UK has a focus on putting the children first and conflict second. The group aims to help parents lower legal costs, ease the stress of separation, and help reduce the pain for the whole family. According to the American Grandparents Association (2012), seventy-two per cent of grandparents think being a grandparent is the single most important and satisfying thing in their life.

Nice work if you can get it.

Grandparents are a valuable resource because they have so many stories and experiences from their own lives to share. And kids love to hear what Mum and Dad did when they were little. Oh, were they ever little like us? We just wanna be BIG! Often children will listen to grandparents even when they are not fans of listening to their parents or other adults. Grandparents also offer a link to a child's cultural heritage and family history. This is especially true, of course, when they come from a dual-heritage family. Children understand more of who they are and where they come from through their connection with their grandparents. So it follows that adopted children do need to know something, if at all possible, about their birth family.

Especially during tough times, such as the Covid-19 pandemic which hit the world in 2020, having an extra layer of support can make a big difference in a child's life. I found in my clinical work that close grandparent–grandchild relationships during the teenage years when kids want to 'divorce' their parents are associated with fewer behavioural and emotional problems and fewer social difficulties with peers. Grandparents offer an extra ear when kids need someone to talk to, because sometimes children just find it easier to open up and share their difficulties and problems with one generation removed.

Grandparents may also offer an affordable childcare option. Well, if they are able to without pushing themselves as well as the pushchair and then exhausting themselves. With both parents in many families working outside of the home, it is often the grandparents, particularly grandmothers, who play a vital role in raising today's children. No longer are they sitting in rocking chairs, knitting. Many are still working, and that's what keeps them young, and going. But it may make things trickier. According to the UK's 2010 Census, roughly 2.7 million grandparents provide for the basic needs of a grandchild, while even more take care of their grandchildren on a regular basis. If they are willing and able, having a grandparent act as either an occasional babysitter or a paid childcare provider gives many parents a great sense of comfort, knowing that they are leaving their children in capable and caring hands. But it may take a toll on the grandparents in terms of energy expenditure beyond which they can really manage.

So first we have of course the 'good' grandmother, with some stories about how they have 'survived'. Is this really 'studied carelessness', *sprezzatura* as the Italians have it, or does it involve more subtle adjustments which go on beneath the surface? Interestingly, there was quite a reluctance for 'good grandmothers' to tell their stories, as if the apparent equanimity of that smooth surface might be broken even by talking about it. Many of them, however, found the actual experience less unnerving than they had thought it might be. Did they have small expectations? (There is more about this in Chapter 3.)

Then there are grandmothers as seen in stories (one in particular, *Little Red Riding Hood*, which has fifty-eight versions in different countries), followed by a chapter about the women who either choose not to have children and thus no grandchildren, or have the choice thrust upon them. How do such women manage the societal expectations and what do they do to compensate (if it can be called that) rather than just carry on being in their own way? Is carrying on the gene the only way? Could they be called 'non-practising Grannies'? These stories put flesh on the bones of habit. There are also stories about women's fraught relationships with their own mothers-in-law. It's a multi-faceted business. Maybe there are conclusions, maybe not, but at least we will have had a conversation which is rounded and grounded.

In my time as a child and adolescent psychotherapist, I've seen a lot of unhappy families and have come to understand more and more how history affects what happens in the present, whether we like it or not. Talking sure does help. I myself wrote a memoir, *Pieces of Molly*, to revisit my own ghosts. Those ghosts of the past can rise up and make the present a bit tricky, if not downright impossible. But even quite apparently static conditions can be moved along over time with some thinking and some talking and some changing all round.

So grandmothers from heaven and from 'hell' (or who have experienced hell) will benefit from reading this book, as well as all those in between, including women who have had no children either by choice or because of supremely painful necessity, and thus no grandchildren. This book is written not only with years of professional experience but also with the wish to explore the realities often hidden behind 'the painted scene'. Just like the 'happy happy' pictures on Facebook (now scientifically proven to enhance *un* happiness), even the 'happiest' of grannies might have moments where life doesn't feel so rosy. This book is for them as well as for those who find they don't conform to a stereotype, and those who don't have children anyway so they never experience this particular 'life transition'.

Many of these ideas may be new, or we may only be partially informed of what is involved in the twenty-first century in this way of 'being'. I hope to avoid psychoanalytic terminology only understood by academic readers, as well as a great parade of academic references.

This book is, in a sense, to misquote the artist Paul Klee, a way of taking an idea for a walk: a thought excursion. The ideas may take you, rather than vice versa, or as Ralph Waldo Emerson put it, 'Do not go where the path may lead; go instead where there is no path and leave a trail.' He also reflected about the purpose of life 'not to be happy but useful, honourable, compassionate, to have it make some difference that you have lived and lived well'. I hope to do that here.

CHAPTER 1

Pits and pitfalls

In which we look at the idea of 'the grandmother'— is she like the Heffalump, a made-up creature?

We orient ourselves in the world by telling ourselves stories about who we are. There is an existential internal need for narrative as well as the external narrative. This factor has become clearer and clearer to me while working with families and the 'referred patient' over the years. It has frequently been evident that the 'referred patient'—often an adolescent—carries something which can be unpacked for the whole family, leaving the adolescent less burdened, though they too may still have a part to play. We organise our experience to make sense of our world and this organising strand may well change, from family to family, from culture to culture, from personality to personality. A 'system of propaganda' can be camouflaged as a mixture of upbringing, instruction, and popular culture. A barrier is built between the inevitable pluralism of information; we build a convenient past and end up believing in it. A dialogue goes on between the individual subject and the cultural system—we are self-interpreting animals, weaving a cloth of the stories told.

And so I suggest we think of the story of a granny as being a bit like the story of a Heffalump, the elephant-like, honey-loving creature conjured up by A. A. Milne to torment Winnie the Pooh, the 'Bear of Very Little Brain', who is terrified of losing his honey. This imaginary creature, born out of a lot of cultural assumptions lumped together to form a (usually) sweet 'whole', can be misleading, partially correct, or sometimes downright deceptive. Are there parallels here between the Heffalump and the granny, perhaps?

This chapter examines the concept of 'grannyhood' by comparing the granny with the Heffalump, the almost mythical beast that has stayed with me since my own grandmother read me the childhood classic *Winnie the Pooh*. Is the granny, like the Heffalump, an imaginary creature, impossible to pin down exactly? Does the 'sweetness' around the concept of grandmothers need to be challenged? Can we break out of 'sweetness' and enter into something more complex and nuanced about grandmothers, as mentioned in the preface? We may indeed be aware of the one reality we see while turning a blind eye to the others that exist just behind it.

So off we go, addressing the mythical aspect of 'the grandmother', transitioning from 'illusion' into fact, just like the mother transitions into the grandmother in life.

The drama begins with Pooh's friend, the boy Christopher Robin, announcing to Pooh and Piglet that he has seen a Heffalump. Not to be outdone, Piglet declares that he too has seen the imaginary creature. Then, of course, terrified of being left out, Pooh reports his own sighting. And being a Bear of Very Little Brain, he starts to fear for his beloved honey. So Pooh hatches a plan to catch their very own Heffalump—a tricky job when no such creature exists. To make matters worse, Piglet is consumed by envy that he didn't come up with the idea first. But the friends put their heads together to come up with the idea of digging a 'deep pit' and enticing the Heffalump with a jar of honey at the bottom of the pit. What can go wrong?

Much as the tale of the Heffalump triggers mixed emotions among Pooh and his friends, so someone who is about to be a grandmother can experience a rollercoaster of feelings, including some apprehension about being 'good enough' for the role, a theme we consider further in the next chapter when we look at the different nuances of grand-motherhood around the world.

If we examine things close up to see the fine grain of individual events rather than looking simply at larger patterns of what people generally think, what do we see? Does the very elastic concept of grannyhood contain within it deep truths about human desire, conflict, and self-deception, much as we see with Pooh and his friends? Are there stories here that do not get told?

We can see that the idea of 'a grandmother' can take on all sorts of different complexions, depending on the early histories of a child's parents and even grandparents. It was Selma Fraiberg and her colleagues who talked of the 'ghosts in the nursery', where present-day actors may be functioning from 'a tattered script', referring to something that happened in the past, and this may well include parents and grandparents. What is in the past must stay in the past—at least, that is what we may hope. But people often fear that the mistakes of the past will be repeated, and indeed they might. In fact, the more conscious these fears are, the smaller is the likelihood of their being repeated in compulsive ways. As Freud said, 'The return of the repressed' can hopefully be avoided. What he was flagging up here is that things are better talked about—if they are repressed, they will return eventually, and sometimes in much more difficult ways. Would it be better for the grandmother to voice her worries about her new role? Should she make her tumult of feelings known to those around her?

As with Pooh and Piglet, envy is fairly often a potent ingredient in the mix when we look at the concept of grannyhood. So who might be envying whom, and why? Does the granny envy her son's attachment to his wife, which of course overrules his attachment to her, as it should do? Does the daughter-in-law envy the son–mother relationship and wish to deny it?

Envy is a form of hostile worship and can turn admiration into resentment. As the celebrated psychoanalyst Melanie Klein says in her 1957 paper 'Envy and gratitude', Chaucer saw envy as the deadliest of the seven deadly sins, while Dante called it the 'radix malorum': root of all evil. Shakespeare knew a lot about it too. The sins—pride, covetousness, lust, envy, gluttony (including drunkenness), anger, and sloth—were held to be transgressions that caused the death not of the body but of the soul. Enough of history maybe, but, although Shakespeare does not address directly the catalogue of deadly sins, he does have much to say on each individual offence. Consider Henry VI: 'When Envy breeds unkind division / There comes the ruin. There begins confusion.'

Tellingly, from the suggestions made in this book, from Sonnet Forty-two, 'Thou dost love her because thou knowest I love her', we see a common human emotion: you want what I've got. Can we detect envy here for the granny, not so far from the surface? The past moves heavily inside us, and the ground may shift as new relationships are made and confusion abounds. Unkind division may be the sad result of thoughts that remain repressed, so Freud wasn't so wrong. We may have moved on from many of the ideas he espoused, but they were the starting point for where we are now.

If we stay with this idea for a little while, we find out that there's no word for envy in primitive cultures, so deeply repressed as it was. Now, although we no longer frown on actions which may generate envy (such as happy social media pictures, which can be particularly envy provoking, and indeed 'science' has proved this), we may silently turn our backs on it when we see it right at the heart of our endeavours. Although we may tend to think of a 'mediator', often the grandmother, as someone who can sort out all these tangles, this may or may not be the way that different people in the drama see it. Even the richest and most glamorous of people have internal models which they may not be living up to, suffering as it were from 'a deficiency of being'. Could it be that the grandmother feels she cannot match the model she imagines for herself? We could perhaps be seen as 'mimic women' (and men)—as there is now less and less real need in our mainly affluent societies, there is more and more desire: they act in relationship with one another.

As René Girard, the so-called Prophet of Envy, said: 'The construction of our beliefs and our identity cannot but have strong mimetic components.' We want what we see others having and enjoying, and grieve its lack in our own lives. This can be especially true in relation to not being allowed to be a functioning grandparent, being excluded from the relationship with the grandchild, for whatever reason (see Chapter 6).

So as I hope I've suggested here, the grandmother (or nan or granny or whatever she may be called) can be likened to the Heffalump, a fantasy creature, made up of hopes and fears, which lie at the bottom of the 'deep pit' inside the mind of each person. This 'story' will be made up of memories, of cultural norms, of current personality, of expectations, both great and small. You can't catch a Heffalump, you can't catch a grandmother, but this book will have a go at making sense of what we have and where we are so that we can laugh at the stereotypes and achieve a bit more clarity on the idea of the grandmother.

CHAPTER 2

Grandmothers round the world

In which some of the accepted international tropes get a look-in—are there differences as well as similarities with white Western notions?

Here I look at the granny in various cultures around the world. This is not an exhaustive list, nor is it designed to be, but it shows that white Western values aren't the only yardstick. This tour of different cultures provides us with a rough map of how to navigate the complex nature of grandmother 'reality' around the world, both in clinical work and in life. Without looking at wider issues beyond Grandmotherland (for instance, political situations), are there common themes and common dreams here? Are grandmothers universally revered or do they have different roles in different parts of the world? Are they sometimes deferred to? Sometimes marginalised? Let's see if you can come to your own conclusions from considering 'how things are' in different regions across the globe. From Australia to Israel and Palestine, via New Zealand, East and Southeast Asia, the Caribbean, South America, South Africa, and Europe, the delusion of 'really knowing' about any subject and being in a position to evaluate it and judge it can be easily maintained if it has cultural respectability. Are there cross-cultural themes here and do they help maintain the 'myth' or provide something more nuanced?

It's important to give adequate thought to the culturescape in each country around this progression from being a mother to being a grandmother. This chapter, then, looks at the cultural assumptions made about grannies around the world. Some of these assumptions are obvious, lying above ground for everyone to see. Others, like truffles, require a bit of digging, as the truffle grows under the ground, enmeshed often in the roots of the cultural tree. As nineteenth-century philosopher Arthur Schopenhauer said, 'All truth passes through three stages. First, it is ridiculed, second, it is violently opposed. Third it is accepted as self-evident.' In terms of grannies, from the icy north to the sun-drenched south, where are we now?

Australia

This section is longer because it describes two rather different ways of 'being': the indigenous way and the Western 'norm'. Let's start with the indigenous population of this huge country, where its original inhabitants faced many challenges, both physically and culturally.

Indigenous societies, close knit and well ordered for tens of thousands of years, became fragmented over time and fragile lands were degraded by the overgrazing of introduced cattle. Christian missions ('the mish') provided sanctuaries, shelters, and food, but also imposed belief systems which repressed traditional practices. This contributed to further unravelling of indigenous societal bonds. In addition, government policies and practices pushed Aborigines and their culture to the brink of extinction.

Between 1940 and 1960, under the Australian government's 'assimilation' policy, which aimed to 'rehabilitate' Aboriginal people for inclusion in European society, a number of programmes were implemented. One was the establishment in the Central Desert region of a number of Aboriginal-only communities alongside those already set up by the Christian missionaries. When people were rounded up from their tribal lands, little consideration was given to the effect of forcing those of different tribal heritages to live in close proximity. Travel restrictions meant that people could not visit their home areas for important cultural activities, to gather foods, or simply for the pleasure or choice of so doing. In one instance the Warlpiri people from Yuendumu were transported around a thousand kilometres to the north to form the community of Lajamanu. The entire community walked back to their Warlpiri homelands three times before the birth of children in Lajamanu led to it being accepted as a permanent home for these wandering people.

Another programme was the removal of non-full-blood children from their homes to be brought up in foster homes or orphanages (forty years later this would be the subject of a major inquiry). A detailed study by Anne Maree Payne in 2021 addressed the question of why the mothers of the 'stolen' children elected not to speak to the investigators involved in the national inquiry that resulted in the 1997 'Bringing Them Home' report. It takes great courage and trust to speak about such elementally painful experiences. Whatever its rationale, in the policy of the day, Aboriginal mothers were undeniably represented as lacking the fitness to raise their children. Many of them were 'stolen' children themselves whose own experiences of being parented in some instances included abuse and racism. (As we observe elsewhere, the abuse flows down the generations.)

And so with all these challenges it fell to grandmothers, who have always been central to the business of rearing future generations, to bind communities together.

It is a remarkable story of survival and adaptation through a destructive period that exceeded any challenges indigenous communities had faced in the central Australian desert in the previous sixty thousand years or more—physical and psychological. 'We somehow all managed to survive,' said an established artist and former child resident of Papunya, a small indigenous community in the Northern Territory.

Later, well-meaning reformists believed that Western education was the answer. There is now a broad consensus that indigenous students need to be taught English to fully participate in society. Most people also agree that indigenous languages need to be preserved, but issues of funding arise. The debate around how to address the language needs of children is confusing, but it has been pointed out that English-only schoolrooms reduce the chances that indigenous languages will survive much longer. The loss of language is devastating for an oral culture that depends on its language for storytelling (by grandmothers) and keeping their tradition and history, their ways of being, alive. Nevertheless, there are some revivals of certain languages and the landscape of a traditionally oral culture is being transformed by a rapidly expanding population of exciting young indigenous writers.

To observe, you also have to be able to listen. There is also the question of listening to what cannot be verbalised. There is a word in most indigenous languages that refers to a very quiet reflective listening to others and oneself. Let's listen to a story highlighting the importance of the grandmother in Aboriginal culture.

An Aboriginal story

My nan's house, to me, was my safe place and symbolises my sense of belonging. Aboriginal people always return home, to their safe place. The home is where it all begins: the meeting place, community gathering, getting together and supporting each other.

Where I grew up there were these 'marker' trees, you knew where you were if you used these marker trees. These trees also had a variety of bush tucker and healing medicines that we used. They were so important to our community, helping us as a life source and also to heal from sickness and other ailments. Community healing is symbolised by these trees.

Positive and loving relationships are the foundation of the next generation. Parents standing and walking together on a positive path, with grandparents behind them, or inside them. Relationships help our community and our people, and stand as a symbol of reconciliation and strength. The sun is the life source, important for regeneration, also the care and nurturing needed for regeneration.

The sun is an important symbol to Aboriginal people, central to our flag. We rely on the sun to provide us with comfort and warmth, but also to grow our foods, herbs, and medicines. The roots are streaming down to the community. Grounding the community, giving them stability, support and structure. From the grandparents, from the great-grandparents.

As we were growing up, our elders taught us kids important lessons, stories, and cultural customs, about the family. In turn, though, the children through their learning and asking questions taught the elders things as well. This cross-learning and sharing is important to the functioning of our community and the continuation of our culture, and grandparents are a vital part of this learning.

The power of art

On a positive note, art would soon become the focus of an important development in the lives of many indigenous women. Through their joyous art and craft works, as widely varied as the lands of central Australia themselves, there was both a resurgence of traditional values and media and newer styles as women started to find their voice. Today, many of them in their seventies and eighties are supporting their communities and they and their art play a major part in helping their people. These artist elders, most usually grandmothers, serve as role models and inspire new-generation artists to fulfil their potential to earn money, which contributes to dealing with the many problems Aborigines in remote rural communities still face. These problems include how to provide within their communities for those young people who do not go off to school in the cities for the week or the term. And so it falls to grandmothers to help with the upbringing of this next generation.

In the many art communities dotted throughout remote rural Australia, indigenous art is still typically segregated, the men working quietly on their sacred objects, the women's rooms hives of activity—and storytelling.

The meaning of family

So the definition of 'family' within Aboriginal communities and culture is distinctly different from the Anglo-Australian nuclear family model. With an emphasis on 'marker trees' and healing herbs, Aboriginal family structures are characterised by collective parenting models which involve both immediate and extended family members (traditionally the term 'grandmother' is extended to include senior women who do not have children of their own—see Chapter 4) and a strong sense of place. This therefore necessitates the engagement of broader family networks in the decisions around the care and protection of Aboriginal children. The 'safe place', as indicated, is both an external and an internal space, where the individual can feel 'at home'. This is the space which has enabled the indigenous population of Australia to hold on to first principles in a society of increasing change and disruption.

Grandparents have always played an important role in family life in the rest of Australia too, but over the last twenty years many have taken on increased responsibility for their grandchildren due to changes in families and in society.

The first major change has been in the provision of child care. Grandparents, mostly grandmothers, are the major providers of child care for preschool children, particularly for babies and toddlers, when both their parents are working. Grandparents also help with older children by picking them up from school and caring for them during school holidays. The second change for grandparents, and the one which is associated with more difficult issues in their own lives, is when they have to take full responsibility for bringing up grandchildren because their parents are unable to do so, quite often because of drug or alcohol abuse. The relationship that grandparents have with their grandchildren can also be affected by the divorce and sometimes re-partnering of the parent generation (see Chapter 6). Other children may then be involved and complications abound.

Most grandparents look forward to the birth of a grandchild, especially the first grandchild, and the pleasure of getting to know the child without the responsibility that being a parent involves. Many grandparents have fulfilling relationships with their grandchildren, watching them learn and grow and being part of their lives, although others find that they are expected to do too much. These expectations can cause friction in the heart of the generational relationships. Some have to bring up their grandchildren when the parents cannot, and some do more childminding than they had expected. Some grandparents have less contact than they would like, due to the parents separating or divorcing (again see Chapter 6).

In developed countries like Australia, grandparents live longer and are generally better educated and healthier than in previous generations. (So no more sitting in the rocking chair, knitting with frail fingers, then.) Some become grandparents when they are relatively young and still in the workforce, whereas others, due to the trend of couples choosing to wait to have their first child, may be retired or approaching retirement, although they may still do some part-time work, which keeps them curious and active. The grandparent role changes over time as grandchildren grow, other grandchildren are born, family members marry, separate, remarry, and move away, and grandparents grow old and very often frail.

When the first child is born, the parents have to adjust to their new roles as parents, to a changed relationship with each other, and to meeting the needs of the new baby. Grandparents, on the other hand, appear to have less adjustment to make because it is of a different nature and less dramatic. And yet, as we have seen earlier, the change involves some profound reflection, reorientation, and behaviour change. Being both a parent and a grandparent can lead to some ambiguity at times. In the beginning, the parent role may be the dominant one as the new grandparents watch the inexperienced parents trying to cope. Nevertheless, the feelings that grandparents have for their own child and those, however loving, that they have for a grandchild are usually appreciably different. Grandparents often worry more about their own child than they do about their grandchild, for whom they generally feel less responsible.

Secure attachment bonds to parents, vital for evolutionary development when the baby is so helpless, are seen as vital for children's emotional growth, but less attention is given to attachment relationships with other significant family members, a tendency that is more part of the Western norm than in other parts of the world. Yet there are many advantages for children in having attachments with strong bonds, which develop over time, to a number of significant adults, and especially to grandparents. Contact with grandparents can be mutually satisfying for both generations. Grandparents are usually not so caught up with the daily routines and have more time to listen, observe, and attend to small things than busy parents. Grandparents can reflect and pass on to their grandchildren cultural knowledge as well as family and community traditions. Positive relationships with grandchildren are not only satisfying for the grandparents but also offer opportunities for emotional integration rather than self-absorption in their later life development.

Contact between grandparents and grandchildren is not entirely a matter of choice, of course, but depends on such aspects as physical proximity, the ongoing relationship that they have with their own children, and demands on their time from other parts of their families. Still, technological advances such as FaceTime can make the world seem a small space. Where the relationship between parents and grandparents is difficult or tenuous, it may not be easy for grandparents to have an ongoing close and loving relationship with the grandchildren (see again

Chapter 6). However, some grandparents choose to play a more symbolic role and may only see their grandchildren at family gatherings such as Christmas and birthdays.

Grandparents may have different relationships with different families of grandchildren for the above reasons, but also because of the age and sex of the grandchildren. At times, grandparents achieve satisfaction with their role through selective investment in a particular grandchild or with one particular family of grandchildren. Where grandparents have too much responsibility for grandchildren, the role may lose its 'magical elements' and, as we have said, friction may grow.

In addition, political, societal and institutional denial, inaction on racism and poverty, and inadequate government support for these new carers have all been shown to affect poorer, non-white sectors of the population disproportionately.

As we see, the definition of 'family' within Aboriginal communities and culture is distinctly different from the Anglo-Australian white nuclear family model. Aboriginal family structures are characterised by collective models which involve both immediate and extended family members. This therefore necessitates the engagement of broader family networks in the decisions around the care and protection of Aboriginal children, as recognised in the Aboriginal Placement Principles, which aim to preserve and enhance the Aboriginal sense of identity. Meanwhile, in the rest of Australia, there is a danger that societal changes will lead to grandmothers feeling overburdened with the responsibility and expectations around helping out with their grandchildren.

New Zealand

Here is another brief cultural view, from New Zealand. *Kaumātua* are the elders in Māori society and are held in high esteem. They have a variety of roles in their *whanau* (wider family), *hapu* (sub-tribe), and *iwi* (tribe). They are seen to be the storehouses of tribal knowledge, genealogy, and traditions (as with the Aboriginal families in Australia) and act as guardians of *tikanga* (Māori customs). They look after the children— traditionally *kaumātua* looked after them while their parents worked or went away to fight, and often brought up the first grandchild. They offer wise leadership and can help resolve disputes within the community. *Kaumātua* often feature in traditional Māori stories as nurturers of the young and keepers of knowledge. Here is a little story about the passing on of knowledge.

A world of knowledge

Māui, a young boy, was raised by his grandfather, Tamanui-ki-te-rangi. He gained knowledge from his *kuia* (female elders), including the secret of fire and the best way to climb to the sky. So you might think about this as keeping warm in this world and ascending safely to the next.

Grandmother's word

More recently, in the second half of the twentieth century, many Māori moved from their traditional homes into cities for work. This meant that traditional knowledge was not always passed down. So some tribes have started programmes for their *kaumātua* to ensure their knowledge and traditions are passed down. Once again, the grandmother plays a vital role in making sure the heritage is kept alive.

China

The grandmother role was central in the traditional Confucian family structure, but the iconoclastic transformations of the 1949 Cultural Revolution had both an impact and implications for its future form. A new role structure for the grandmother emerged, involving greater complexity, wider options and functions. The role of a grandmother can be understood in each culture as an idiosyncratic blend of gender, social and functional values, as I hope we have already established.

This is the personal view of one Chinese contributor to this book.

> My maternal grandmother is eighty-one years old now. She was a mother with seven children. My mother was her second child. My grandmother usually had to walk hours to school because in her village there was no middle school. My grandmother married my grandfather, whom she had never met before

the marriage, so that her family did not need to support her anymore and could also get some money from her husband's family so she could finish her schooling. In the last year of her middle school, she was pregnant. Then she graduated and had a baby. At that time women were encouraged to have more children as so many men had died in the war. So in the family, she had seven in total.

For the first three children, in my mother's memory, my grandmother didn't really know how to be a mother. My mother's grandmother came to help a lot. My bad-tempered grandfather occasionally hit the children and my grandmother did not dare to protect them. My grandparents were together until my grandpa died twenty years ago. It's difficult to tell if they really had romantic love towards each other (unlikely, we might surmise?) because they had not even met before they married.

Overall, my grandmother is still a very energetic woman. She used to be the female basketball team leader in school and was good at maths, and she taught both to me. Since our generation grew up, she comes to visit us in various countries. I love her very much!

Another correspondent chose to describe an old Chinese story about a grandmother called 'Wolf Grandmother'. It differs a bit from Little Red Riding Hood's story (see Chapter 6 for more on Little Red Riding Hood) and this is how the story goes in the Chinese version.

Wolf Grandmother

In the early Jin Dynasty (1115 to 1234), there was a family with a father, mother, and three children. The father went to join the army and the mother made and sold clothes in the market. One day, the mother went to the city market to sell cloth and the three children stayed at home. The mother told the children not to open the door to strangers, but not long after she left, the Wolf came. The Wolf disguised itself as a grandmother and used various tricks to fool the three children to open the door.

In the beginning, the Wolf Grandmother was also 'responsible' and took good care of her three children. But in the middle of the night, the oldest sister seemed to hear grandma eating so, she asked grandma, 'What are you eating?'

'I'm eating peanuts,' said grandma.

'Can I have some?' said the sister.

Grandma was silent, as if she was thinking, and the noise of eating stopped.

Absent parents

As a background to the story, we can see that the father was absent in the army and the mother was no doubt stressed looking after three children all on her own. The mother might be an idealised figure for the child, a figure who cannot be attacked or turned bad in the child's mind. So in fantasy, the grandmother could turn into a horrifying figure, as bad as a wolf (see Chapter 6).

The story may represent the Chinese phenomenon of the absent father. While in the past the father needed to join the army, more recently many fathers in the countryside have gone to the cities to work, leaving the children at home with their mother.

Role of grandparents

The grandparents are involved much more in looking after grandchildren compared with Western grandparents. Especially after the one-child policy instituted in China in the 1980s, couples in this generation have parents and parents-in-law who want to be involved in looking after this one precious child.

My Chinese contributor followed on from the story of the Wolf Grandmother with personal recollections of her own grandmother.

> My grandmother is a robust figure. She was born into a poor family and her parents asked her to marry my grandfather in order to get some money from my grandfather when my grandmother was only thirteen years old. When she was sixteen, she gave birth to her first child and then she had seven children in thirteen years.
>
> When I was three, I was sent to my grandmother's place because my eyesight was not good and needed to be treated in the hospital in the city, but my parents joined the army in the town. My grandmother looked after me for a year and I formed

a strong attachment to her. Perhaps, I also kept her as a warm and robust woman figure inside my mind, but of course it also created some confusion for a small child to understand emotionally: why had my mother left me there? My parents took me home again when I was four.

Interestingly, in China, we now have another name for a type of mother: the Tiger Mother. This describes a mother who is very competitive and harsh with her children. She wants her child always to be the best. I think, perhaps it is also a bit like the Wolf Grandmother who ate the children? Maybe tiger mothers also 'eat' their children's creativity and autonomy? They are unwilling to allow separation, as if the children are still part of their body, so maybe eating in this sense means getting them back into their bodies? This means there is very little room for grannies to play a part.

Taiwan

In a 2009 study by Sandel, Cho, Miller, and Wang, researchers interviewed sixteen grandmothers of three year olds. The study looked at Euro-American and Taiwanese folk theories of grandmothers' roles in discipline and advice giving. All the grandmothers who participated perceived their role as distinct from that of mothers, but, when it came to their interpretations of the tasks that were expected of them, their views differed.

Euro-American grandmothers saw their role as a companion to their grandchildren. They did not see themselves as disciplinarians and found it problematic when it came to giving advice. Meanwhile, Taiwanese grandmothers saw themselves primarily as temporary caregivers, and they were more than prepared to discipline their grandchildren if they misbehaved and to give their daughters-in-law advice. Now there is a difference in point of view—in other cultures that might well relegate the granny to the 'bad' category (see Chapter 7).

Results of this study contribute to the overwhelmingly clear finding that grandmothers' roles are culture specific, leading to different understandings of the family unit. This goes against the grain of the 'official' white Western wisdom in many cases, as we have seen.

Japan

Now we make a move from traditional indigenous culture to the situation in modern Japan and here we have a different set of factors to consider. Middle-aged grandmothers who participate in their daughters' *Satogaeri bunben* (first delivery) show significantly reduced levels of self-esteem after childbirth compared with before childbirth. They may worry: if they were important before childbirth, what happens afterwards? Are they going to be displaced?

Grandmothers play a significant role in supporting their daughters at the grandparents' house before the first delivery. This is a typical event in modern Japan, but here again there is a confounding factor. Grandmothers, especially those in middle age (regarded as less than sixty years old), who support their daughters in this way, suffer with this lower self-esteem after the birth, indicating that *Satogaeri bunben* is a burden for this age bracket.

Again, this finding seems unsurprising, as younger grandmothers are working outside as well as inside the home—a dual burden which might indeed cause anxiety and a lowering of self-esteem. Reitzes and Mutran reported that self-esteem in middle-aged working women is correlated in part with a person's sense of commitment to adult roles and identity, as they identify with both their work and family roles. In comparison with the older age bracket, the middle-aged grand-mothers showed significantly higher percentages of employment and daily care for family members and lower percentages participating in regular hobbies and volunteering activities, suggesting that they might play important roles in home duties as a mother and as a working adult.

In the case of *Satogaeri bunben*, a grandmother needs to live with her daughter and her grandchild/grandchildren for a long time, something which automatically increases the burden of housework, such as preparing meals and washing clothes for the family during the perinatal period. Therefore, the burden on the grandmother increases. As a result, support for grandmothers who take care of their daughters before childbirth is necessary in order to reduce such burdens, especially among middle-aged grandmothers. Other family members and community support may reduce these other burdens.

Gerard, Landry-Meyer, and Roe reported that professional assistance and community services were important in minimising the negative impact of child-related challenges on grandparents' wellbeing. A relatively new phenomenon in Japan is the 'child-care salon', offering parental support from older people in the community. Kusano, Ono, and Hayakawa found that a higher frequency of child-care salon participation reportedly reduces child care-related stress.

Although there is more involvement in Japan between mother and daughter when a grandchild enters the picture than may be found in the typical Western scenario, there is also a greater sense of burden, something we will find below when we look at the Philippines and Guyana.

The Philippines

Family is considered to be the foundation of social life for most Filipinos. There is the core family unit, but bonds are often tightly knit among extended family members (see Australia's Aboriginals). People may be encouraged to have a relationship with their aunts and uncles that is just as strong as the relationship with their parents. This is something that those from Western nuclear families may find difficult to comprehend.

Close 'family' relationships often go beyond one's genetic connections or bloodlines to incorporate distant relatives, close neighbours, or friends. For example, it is common to hear people refer to distant relatives or non-relatives with familial terms such as *tita* (aunt), *tito* (uncle), *lola* (grandmother), and *lolo* (grandfather).

Filial devotion is an important concept in Filipino culture. It is understood as essential in order to maintain the collective unity of the family. Many Filipinos believe that each family member has several duties and responsibilities they must uphold. Observing one's duties and responsibilities is important in order to correctly respect others and to ensure continuity among family members. As a Filipino contact said to me, 'Grannies are there for joy, not babysitting.' Here, duty takes second place, and feelings of joy are considered much more important. Family members are required to show respect to their elders at all times—again, rather different from the white Western 'norm'. The opinions of younger family members and children are considered to be secondary to those of their superiors. Moreover, as they age, older people are nearly always taken care of by their children or grandchildren.

In a Filipino household, it's quite common to find three generations living together. Grandparents frequently play a significant role in raising their grandchildren. Extended family will often live relatively close to one another and will come together during large celebrations.

Since the 1970s, the Philippines has been exporting labour, with some people engaging in paid labour abroad while others remain in their home town or village. This means that many Filipino families are spread across the world, something I came across frequently in my work in the Family Centre. It is also common to find families in the Philippines that have some members who return to their family home during weekends after spending a week in major cities for work or study. Filipino society has widely adapted to the change in family structure. Some parents will leave their children in the Philippines while they seek work abroad in order to better support their family left behind. In turn, they send money back to their parents or siblings who have been given the duty of caring for the children. It is common to find aunts, uncles, and godparents taking care of their nieces, nephews, or godchildren by sending money home to pay for their education, a situation that is unfamiliar among most Western families but is common in countries like Guyana.

Those living abroad will attempt to see their family once a year, returning home to the Philippines during their break from work in another country. This can be particularly difficult for those with children or elderly parents. In order to support their families, Filipinos abroad will send a *balikbayan box*, containing various items such as clothing, household objects, and gifts for their family. In my family work, I encountered many Filipino mothers who came to the UK in order to support their families but in so doing created a rupture in the attachment relationships with their children. Nevertheless, those children were culturally adapted to such rupture, which seems extreme and difficult to those used to a Western nuclear family way of thinking about what is 'normal'. Still, it can make it trickier when the parents go back home or the adolescent children join them, as I found again in family meetings. In one such series of meetings, the mother and adolescent daughter could only relate to what was happening between them via a TV soap opera popular at the time, rather than linking it to their own situation, although this was happening at an unconscious level. It felt important to me to respect their defences and the work proceeded, with some success in their relationship.

Guyana

There are five races living side by side in Guyana: Amerindian, Portuguese, African, East Asian, and Chinese. Among them, some mothers hand their children into the care of their grandmothers; some grandmothers have to both nurture and discipline their grandchildren (here the discipline issue is very different from the Western model, in which grandmothers take second place after the parents in terms of setting rules); and some grandmothers are expected to provide financial support from their meagre pensions or salary. It is estimated that about twenty-seven per cent of children in Guyana are raised directly by grandmothers and a significant number of them are being supported indirectly by grandparents.

Most grandmothers here are not young women. Many of them do not have well-paying jobs, and quite a few are retired. Many are not capable of running behind their very active grandchildren and therefore cannot keep track of all of them. Their homes are veritable nurseries supported by their meagre incomes.

In spite of the many serious challenges most grandmothers here face, they fulfil their responsibilities to take care of their grandchildren with impressive courage and resolve, even though they may receive little support from their own children and often nothing from the fathers of the grandchildren.

The stress most grandmothers encounter in taking care of their grandchildren from neonates to full-grown adults would overwhelm the average parent. These brave grandmothers, willing to make the necessary sacrifices, are the backbone of Guyanese society. They are the ones who end up raising and nurturing so many of Guyana's children to become productive and law abiding citizens.

On the positive side, grandmothers are trying to provide a home, food, clothes and an education for many children—this is indeed a celebration of the elders. On the negative side, some cannot even provide for themselves, yet they are thrust into the demanding and difficult role of parenting at a point in their lives when times are much tougher for them. In contrast, it seems only a few grandfathers have taken on the role of parenting their grandchildren, but that is another story, as yet untold.

Most of us have fond memories of our grandmothers (as do I—I will explore this in Chapter 8). They are a special breed of women who have mellowed with age but possess a wealth of experience and knowledge that society could draw on to raise and nurture children and build a better future. They are the silent and unsung heroes within Guyanese society, making this society stronger than it might otherwise be today. We tend to love our grandmothers, but most of the time we see them in a stereotypical old-fashioned way—grandmothers are expected to be calm, collected, have an outdated style, and spend their days baking and knitting. Society's narrow perception that older women shouldn't dress up, wear bright colours, and go on dates is primitive. National Gorgeous Grandma Day, celebrated annually on July 23rd, intends to dispel this mindset and encourage people not to frown upon women over the age of fifty who are not yet ready to retire to a quiet life.

In 1984 Alice Solomon graduated from Guyana's Wellesley College at the age of fifty. She realised that society saw her and other women of her age as senior citizens, regardless of whether or not they were actual 'grandmothers'. Determined to challenge this way of thinking, she came up with the idea of 'Gorgeous Grandma'. Women who were apparently 'beyond their expiration date' and no longer relevant are termed as 'grandmas', so Solomon decided to embrace the term but amped it up with the use of the word 'gorgeous'. Gorgeous Grandma is all about presenting a cooler image of older women in Guyana and eliminating stereotypes which confine them to a limited box.

The Caribbean

As we continue in the Caribbean, it's important to be clear at the outset about the meaning here of 'the nuclear family'. It is generally defined as two parents (usually a mother and a father but also two mothers or two fathers) and dependent children living under one roof, committed to one another and the family unit. This is considered to provide strength and stability, greater behavioural success and educational support.

A particularly interesting article written in 2020 by Leighan Renaud considers the Caribbean family, looking first at the history of family life. Renaud points to the centrality of women in family life in the Caribbean and the prevalence of a matrifocal family structure. The article concludes that misunderstanding and vilification of alternative family structures, rooted in history, still exist, asking: What models of love and support do we miss if we cling to the model of the nuclear family? Whose contributions to family life get forgotten if we use only linear family trees?

My own son's former girlfriend, African Caribbean through and through even though she was born and lives in the North of England, is an insightful woman who runs the Afro-Caribbean Health Network. She says,

> My mother was born on the tiny Caribbean island of Carriacou, a sister island of Grenada, with a population of six thousand. We have traced her maternal lineage back to her great-grandmother, who was born into slavery. Given major gaps in the archives, hers is a history that would be difficult to trace through archival documentation.
>
> Ours is a very big family and it is clear that the traditional family tree wouldn't honour these networks of love, mainly created and maintained by women.

Understanding the Caribbean focus on the maternal line, an issue that is not central to the Western norm, and moving away from the linear 'nuclear' family gives us an insight into the 'dysfunction' of the post-slavery Caribbean family structure, its complexities, its resilience, how it has evolved, and how it definitely does not conform to Eurocentric white colonial ideals.

Brazil

In Brazil, contrary to the general trend in Western countries, grand-mothers have more power than mothers in deciding what happens with the children. So it is no wonder that they are celebrated in style. Whereas some countries hold beauty contests, choosing from beautiful girls most worthy of wearing an honorary title, in Brazil you will find another of the surprising contests we encountered above under Guyana: 'Miss Grandmother of Brazil'. There are only two prerequisites for the participants: they must be beautiful and they must be grandmothers. One can point out that there is a genetic factor, but looking at pictures from the competition, we can safely say that the participants spend a lot of time in the gym and jogging.

One of the winners of the 'Miss Grandmother of Brazil' title was Maria Lucia, at the age of forty-nine. She was already a grandmother twice over, but this did not prevent her from being photographed in a bikini, with her chiselled body adorned with tattoos and navel piercings.

One woman offered this contribution: 'Many Brazilian people consider that grannies double the benefits of parents because of the care they provide to the grandchildren, offering love and freedom, which will generate good memories in the future, on both sides. I have an example from my family. My sister's husband died last February. She has a grand-daughter, nearly three years old, who has given her the will to carry on living. The little girl is brilliant, so tender, and very attached to my sister.' Grannies are valued indeed.

South Africa

And so we turn to the benefits of fitness in old age, in particular looking at the case in South Africa.

In Johannesburg, there is a trend among grandmothers to take up boxing to keep fit and fight off some of the ailments of old age. Despite the tough nature of the sport, women over the age of sixty-five have been keen to participate. Constance Ngubane, a sprightly eighty-three-year-old, said that they are trying to find ways to curb the burden of chronic diseases like diabetes through boxing. 'We were invited at the gym to train. We agreed because we wanted to be healthier. We wanted to exercise our muscles and not continue doing nothing at home.'

Four African authors from the University of Witwatersrand conducted research into factors influencing regular physical exercise among the elderly in residential care facilities in South African health districts. Regular exercise in the elderly has proved to enhance gait and balance, leading to a reduction in the incidence of falls.

Clara Mose, sixty-nine, said her doctor had recommended she join a boxing club. 'I was attending physiotherapy sessions at Helen Joseph

Hospital when I first heard about the gym. The nurses at Helen Joseph Hospital recommended that it would be best for me to go to the boxing gym at Cosmo City. The gym offers two sessions a week, including cardio and boxing exercises.'

One of the grannies said her fitness journey started after being diagnosed with osteoporosis. 'I used to be very sick before I started boxing. I had sore knees and a painful back. I couldn't move or do anything when my back became painful.'

While the boxing gym has helped the elderly community stay active and motivated, the next step is to guide the boxing grannies on how to eat a healthy balanced diet. This is of course also a vital clue to longevity. And all of this is helping grandmothers stay active and involved with their grandchildren for much longer.

Czech Republic

The following was written by one of my contributors.

Babička (*The Grandmother*) by Božena Němcová is a Czech classic, written in 1855. It is compulsory reading in schools even today. That it has not lost its popularity is evidenced by the fact that it has had three thousand editions and been translated into twenty-two languages. Quite a record indeed.

The events take place when Bohemia was still part of the Austro-Hungarian Empire. German was the official language, but it was also the epoch of the awakening of Czech nationalism, when authors began to write in Czech.

Written shortly after the death of Němcová's son, the book depicts village life as she herself had known it. With our insights today, might we say that it was a form of therapy for her? There is much emphasis now on journalling as a way of coming to terms with what has happened in the past. Perhaps Němcová was one of the first people to recognise this as a way to process traumatic events.

The story is told through the eyes of one of the grandchildren and depicts village life through the various seasons as well as the social order of the time. We gradually learn about the social position of women of different ages and the importance of the grandmother as carer and transmitter of culture.

The heroine, Babička, is the epitome of wisdom, piety, and goodness. She comes to live in the village of Staré Bělidlo at the invitation of one of her daughters, Terézka, who is married to the head groom of the prince's estate, By then Babička is a widow; her soldier husband had died in the war. She helps in the household, mainly by looking after her four grandchildren. They become her constant companions and she is their beloved grandmother, always ready to tell them stories as well as instil them with her high moral principles. However, she also has fun with them. She soon becomes very popular in the village and her diligence and good deeds gain her the favour of the local princess.

Babička gets up early in the morning, feeds all the animals, then wakes the childen and they spend the days together. She loves baking and her products are much appreciated. On one of the outings, when Babička and the children visit the gamekeeper's house, they meet the princess, who invites them to her castle. The grandchildren are overcome by the splendour of the rooms. Babička so impresses the princess with her wisdom that she becomes a frequent visitor at the castle. Babička does not exploit this for herself but she is ready to help others. When one of her acquaintances comes to Babička, desperate for help because her lover is due to join the army for fourteen years, Babička goes to the princess on her behalf and the lover is released.

Babička's stories were mostly accounts from her own life, one of which was the story of a young woman called Viktoria. A renowned beauty, she fell in love with an unknown soldier with whom she ran away and was never heard of again. Some time later, a mad woman with a child started wandering in the forest and despite many attempts, no one was able to get close to her. Eventually this woman was recognised—here was Viktoria! But she threw her child into a sluice and she herself was killed by lightning. Undoubtedly the moral of the story was that sin will be punished.

We follow Babička through the seasons and the growing up of the grandchildren until her death. Baruška, her favourite granddaughter, has left for the city to study but comes back from time to time. Following a rather harsh winter Babička succumbs and dies, but not before Baruška returns to see her. Babička is mourned by the whole village, including the princess who watches the funeral cortege and is heard to say, 'There goes a happy woman.'

Babička is representative of the culture and mores, the social order, and the position of women in society at that time. Anecdotally, until the Second World War, it is said that many families had grandparents in the countryside, so that children could spend their long summer holidays with them. Changes later took place with the onset of communism and again in the current post-communist era.

In most countries, including the Czech Republic, grandmothers were the transmitters of childrearing culture, passing on the ideas about grandmothers and their role.

Expectations

What follows is based on the article 'Being a good grandmother: the normative expectations'. Aha, here we have 'the norm' again.

Although historically grandparents have played a key role in the Czech family, societal changes show that grandmothers are perhaps rethinking their role and the expectations from parents over that role are also changing. Nevertheless, despite demographic changes, the view of devoted grandmothers in Czech society persists. For grandmothers here, caring for their grandchildren is often the most fulfilling aspect of their lives.

One of the key factors that distinguishes Czech families from Western nuclear families is generational interdependence. Many grandmothers gave up their jobs to play a crucial role caring for their grandchildren, thus enabling the mother to return to work after maternity leave. This became especially prevalent after the fall of communism when nursery places were scarce. This meant too that grandmothers had a more active and authoritative role in the family than in Western culture. Nevertheless, interviews with a number of parents and grandparents showed that parents were very clear that they expected grandparents to respect their childrearing methods and not impose their own, in much the same way that Western families operate.

A number of demographic factors seem to have had an influence also, changing current trends around the grandmother's role. People living to a greater age means that grandmothers may have longer with their grandchildren, while shrinking family sizes mean that more time may be devoted to the individual child. The growing divorce rate also has an influence on the role of paternal grandparents, who are playing a diminishing role in the care of their grandchildren.

While some studies show that the changing mother/father role has marginalised the role of the grandmother, other studies show that Czech grandmothers see their role as a continuation of their role as a mother. Yet there are various features which distinguish the roles of mother and grandmother. The parent is a pivotal influence in how the relationship between grandmother and grandchild is mediated. The quality of this relationship will be influenced in no small measure by the quality of the relationship between parent and grandparent. A further factor in the intensity and nature of the contact between grandparent and grandchild will be living conditions and the nature of the parents' partnership.

Culture of ageing

We should also consider the 'culture of ageing', a term that refers to the opportunities for older generations to be involved in many more activities than in the past, among them the University of the Third Age. This shift has brought with it new conflicts, especially for grandmothers struggling to manage the different roles in their lives—parents expect grannies to provide interesting activities for their grandchildren and that they should be available when needed, so grandparents being engaged in other fulfilling activities creates a conflict.

Thus, as the traditional framework has loosened, there is conflict between the expectations of the different phases of the life cycle and maintaining the traditional family ties. Nevertheless, while there is some evidence of the diminishing role of the grandmother in her grandchildren's lives, in other instances, despite contemporary societal changes, these ties are intensified.

Poland

Every year on January 21st, people across Poland take a moment to honour their grandmothers. Grandmother's Day (*Dzień Babci*) was the brainchild of *Kobieta i Życie* (*Woman and Life*) magazine in 1964. A year later, the *Express Poznański* (*Poznań Express*) newspaper began to popularise the new holiday. In 1966, the *Express Wieczorny* (*Evening Express*) joined in and

Grandmother's Day has been celebrated every year since. Grandfather's Day is not forgotten, of course, and is celebrated a day later, on January 22nd.

Grandmother's Day is widely celebrated across the country. It is an occasion for people to show their gratitude and appreciation for these important women in their lives, with small presents, greeting cards, and flowers. Often the gifts will be handmade. Schools and kindergartens sometimes organise events to celebrate the holiday.

Here is a rhyme dedicated to Babcia on Grandmother's Day:

> Czy wiesz moja Babciu kochana,
> Że w myślach moich jesteś od rana?
> Gdy sen z moich oczu zmywałam,
> O życzeniach dla Ciebie myślałam.
> Szukałam dla Ciebie czegoś cennego,
> Aż w końcu znalazłam coś bardzo drogiego.
> Płomień miłości Ci ofiaruję,
> Bo tego ludziom ciągle brakuje.
> Chcę abyś wiecznie szczęśliwa była,
> I sto wiosenek w zdrowiu przeżyła.

> Do you know my dear grandmother,
> That you are in my thoughts since the morning?
> When the sleep from my eyes I was washing,
> About wishes for you I thought.
> I was looking for something valuable for you,
> Until finally I found something very precious.
> I offer you the flame of love,
> Because people often miss it.
> I want you to always be happy,
> And may you live hundred springs in health.
> Grandma our beloved, do not be ever worried,
> Let grateful grandchildren circle, always see you happy!
> Let the healthy years of days flow in prosperity,
> Let your moments of joy be intertwined with your grandchildren's love!
> Grandma is like a good fairy, who opens doors to fairy tales,
> Because when she puts us to bed then we have beautiful dreams.
> Grandma does everything for us, with her help everyone is happy.
> Grandma is terribly loved, so may she live one hundred years!

Israel and Palestine

It seems a good idea to end this chapter with an account of two very disparate countries, close together and even overlapping, where female representatives from the countries are working together to create new solutions and where a grandmothers' group is central to how the situation evolves. This final insight is an example of how socio-political and cultural influences can be reconciled—with grandmothers playing a central role. (For the full story, please read Jillian Slutzker's article at https://pij.org/articles/1379/engaging-grandmothers-israeli-and-palestinian-women-share-their-stories.)

The people of Israel and Palestine have experienced unimaginable losses during Middle Eastern conflict. One Israeli woman had lost her son in the Lebanese civil war. One Palestinian woman had lost her brother when he was shot and killed near her village by the Israeli Defence Force. The same woman's mother and three of her brothers had been imprisoned in Israel for political activism. Yet these two women fought their anger and bitterness and instead chose peace and forgiveness to join their considerable forces, a move that once might have seemed impossible.

The women became founder members of the Parents Forum, working together as bereaved Israeli and Palestinian women, on issues of reconciliation and peace. Their efforts earned them a mention in US President Barack Obama's Middle East speech of 2011.

The initiative evolved into workshops in which sixteen grandmothers from both 'sides' met to try to understand their parallel narratives. Despite never having met before, and resistance on both sides to facing 'the other', they came together to tell their traumatic stories. And over time a level of understanding and empathy developed. The initiative became known as 'The Grannies Project'. As one woman said, 'We are all mothers and grandmothers, all human beings.'

Gradually the barriers came down and bonds were formed—as this woman said, 'It's part of our DNA', which indeed it is. We forget this to our detriment. Both 'sides' bore witness to each other's painful narratives, often for the first time, including a visit to the Holocaust Museum. 'I did not know,' wept one Palestinian woman. So enemies became friends as they shared their collective stories.

At the end of the project, one of the tasks was for the grandmothers to draw their 'dream house'. The resulting pictures were not full of anger and despair but showed children, olive trees, and wells flowing with water. The grannies then returned to their places of origin, taking with them this new understanding. One of the participants said, 'I don't want to live in a state for graves. I don't want to be the mother or grandmother of a dead body.'

Perhaps all we grandmothers, whatever role we play in our grandchildren's lives and wherever we live in the world, would do well to remember the words above: 'We are all mothers and grandmothers, all human beings.'

CHAPTER 3

Happily ever after?

*In which we look at the 'Good Granny' and
her conditional happiness*

I f we accept that one of the most important relationships is that between grandchildren and grandparents (and here we are thinking particularly about grannies), we 'normally' have a positive view. At its best it can be a relationship that gives sheer joy without the tensions which are an inevitable part of the parent/child relationship. But 'Where's that palace whereinto foul things Sometimes intrude not?' asked Othello.

This chapter offers contributions from 'happy grannies' who have found the transition fairly straightforward, or straightforward enough. Why? Is it related to having had happier relationships to grandmothers themselves? Not necessarily, unless the memory morphs over time (see Chapter 7). Or does it also depend on the relationships their own daughters or daughters-in-law had with their mothers and their grand-mothers? How does 'good enough' granny-ing play out in the real world? Adult sons and daughters may be aware and feel guilty about the tensions inherent in their relationships with their children, and may produce the grandchildren in order to give their parents the pleasure that they themselves may be unable to give them in a consistent way. Unrealistic parental expectations may cause regret and then there can be delight at giving the grandparents these newly formed human beings.

Grandparents too may feel relief at being able to give to their grand-children the unconditional love they might have been unable to offer their children. Win win, you might say?

An incomplete world

As children say:

> Grandparents are the backbone of a family, the root of our lives. I wonder what would happen without them?
>
> What would happen with no granny to tell you stories?
>
> The world would really be incomplete.
>
> Grandparents never hesitate to be there for us.

Let's hear from one of my contributors.

> Being a grandparent is the best job in the world, but it's not always easy! Today's kids can be tough to please, and it's hard to fit in with other activities. Too many activities, perhaps? But usually, they will be excited to spend special time with grandma, this quality time focused solely on them, that is sometimes difficult for their parents (who often have the distractions of the house, work and all the demands of a busy young family) to offer. It's a win for grandparents, parents, and the kids too.
>
> But what can do you do that's fun for both grandparents and kids? While I have no intention of being prescriptive, here are a few pointers. Fun is the emphasis here. This isn't the time to aim for perfection. Let the kids be kids. Give each one a special time with grandma (or grandpa). Grandparents teach you to respect other people. Love and good feelings are important: don't pay attention to material things or what people may look like from the outside. My grandparents are beautiful people, so active and so healthy. Even though they are old, they always have a strong desire to enjoy life and offer this enjoyment to their families too.
>
> My four grandparents have a common goal in common in life: to see our family full of happiness and to see us growing up healthy and happy. They want me and my family to have a successful future, so they can prove to themselves that they did a great job raising our parents.

My grandparents are people who are always in tune with new things in the world. For example, my grandmothers always care about fashion, how they dress, and their personal appearance. And my grandfathers always care about economics or important issues in the world. [*Well this is a bit of a gendered split here. Is it possible to have a political granny and a dandy grandad?*]

No one can ever replace people like our grandparents. They can understand our doubts about life because nobody in this world has more experience about life than they have.

Grandparents, then, have always played a vital role in the lives of families, and never more so than today.

The best part of listening to stories by grandparents is that they each have their personal touch. I wonder how they get a new story every day. Grandparents have a Midas touch: their stories take us to a new world, a world of happiness, astonishments, and surprises. Grandchildren love to hear such stories. Stories create a bond between grandparents and grandchildren. Try never to skip a chance to tell a story. Or if your life gets too crowded and busy, you can link them up to 'Granny and Her Friends Read Children's Stories' (https://m.youtube.com/channel/UCp7ma0rlYS4GsYHNHPMuqsA).

Keep hold of the baby books—not your grandchild's but their parents' books. There is nothing children like better than seeing their parents as peers (rather than the people who tell them to clean up their room and it's time for bed). Talk about their mum or dad's first step, first word, anything they did that was naughty or funny.

Whether it's bridge, gin rummy or mahjong, playing games you love with your grandkids opens them up to new experiences and shows them a piece of you and the hobbies you enjoy. What child doesn't love competing against Grandma, or seeing Grandpa make mistakes? 'Sometimes, I purposely mess up,' says one, 'because my grandkids just love it when they catch me out.' It's a small step towards being 'big' and learning to take turns.

Baking with the grandkids is terrific. Okay, yes, there's the yum-yum factor, but the hidden benefits are important, too. Kids like to be included in grown-up activities, and cooking or baking is just that. But it is also about family traditions and history. So while your grandchildren are measuring and stirring, you're teaching them how to plan, follow instructions, and develop patience. You also might be sharing where the recipe came from and how your mother or grandmother used to make it. Knowing these facts goes a long way with kids and they will remember these recipes for their own children.

A lot of bonding can take place even over a video game. Here, kids become the teachers and can show you what they like and how they do things. And if you don't catch on, don't worry. 'Yes, you may be a klutz,' says one granny, 'but that will only make it more fun for the grandkids.' This is sportsmanship with a huge potential laugh factor.

Most children love wearing sweaters knitted by their grandparents. Making patchwork or embroidery on your granddaughter's favourite skirt will be something she'll treasure for a long time.

Encouraging reading? Well, it is educational, of course, and has no downside. It can easily be turned into a ritual kids will love. If your library has a story hour and the kids are younger, take them to that and then go to the children's section and browse. If the grandkids are older, ask them what they're reading, check out a copy for yourself, and start your own mini-book club together.

A jewellery box too is a great source of fun and exploration, like a mini-history of your life. Inside can be wondrous and beautiful items that have interesting stories attached to them. Maybe these things have been passed on from your own grandmother. This is just what kids—especially teens and in particular teenage girls—love. Tell kids about the necklaces, earrings, and bracelets inside your treasure trove. Let them try them on. They'll feel like royalty and will look forward to seeing the jewellery box every time they visit. Same goes for a button box, as each button can tell a story.

Lastly, the most important thing every grandparent can give is their unique experience. Wisdom which grew over time is a boon for grandchildren and will help them want to do something fruitful in their own lives. Every wrong deed you've done and the lessons you've learned will give your grandchildren a lesson for their own lives.

German filmmaker Wim Wenders ascribes his love of reading to his relationship with his grandmother: 'I actually learned to read before I went to school out of sheer necessity because my grandmother couldn't read very well herself. I started to learn by following her finger. I learned by intuition. I learned to recognise words and then read a book a day for years. Now I see my niece and all she wants to do is read. She just wants books. I'm so happy.'

Here's another happy view: the stories that follow are the backbones of our lives. Stories are at the true heart of the project of Being Alive and keep us lively.

What it means to be a granny

An Italian Nonna

For some unfortunate people the word 'granny' conjures up an image of a dithering old dear who 'drops in' on her family at the most inconvenient of times, who comments on the upbringing of her grandchildren, is severely critical, and maybe worst of all she believes the 'internet' to be a modern-age type of fishing tackle.

On the other hand, many working parents see 'granny' as a godsend. She is the one who takes and collects the kids from school, prepares meals, does the housework, shopping, etc. But it's not all work and no play. On the contrary, she enjoys games and 'learning' about the wonders of the latest technological devices that her little ones can use so expertly. Initially (where I live in Tuscany), granny or nonna as she's called in Italy, plays a very important role in the lives of most families, very often living with them (or in a flat/house close by) and cared for even till ripe old age. She is loved and respected, often called upon to give advice and comfort.

Personally speaking, I am Nonna to Edoardo (seven) and Elizabetha (five) and find grandparenthood very rewarding and gratifying, even rejuvenating. (With the exception of trying contorted karate moves or bending and stretching to imitate wild animals!) I see the world through their eyes, with innocence, love, and enthusiasm. Being a teacher, I can't help imparting the knowledge I've acquired during my teaching career. Sometimes I think it's falling on deaf ears. Then the 'magic window' opens and they reveal something you've forgotten and that's really the most fantastic moment that makes being a granny worthwhile.

'Nonna!' Sorry, must go, it's my turn to be shopkeeper and there are two demanding customers to be served. Now doesn't this beat going out to work?

What a happy tale. The children want to be grown up, buying things from the shop. This is a narrative where happiness has been assigned: is it a 'magic window' or does it depend on a number of interrelated issues?

More from Italy

Another Italian view of happy grannyhood emphasises the need to treat the grandchildren as 'intelligent human beings'. 'Don't think they don't understand, they're not stupid.' So the project is one of growing up, buying things is part of the project, and these children are well on their way. 'I adore her. I wish I saw more of her!'

Adoration—something many grannies feel for their grandchildren. The Western Christmas carol *O Come Let Us Adore Him* sums up the feelings many grandparents have for their grandchildren. Adoration of the baby is a perennial theme.

A granny overseas

Here is an account from a granny in the UK whose grandchildren are in Poland.

> I'm not called Granny, I'm called *Babcia*, warmly embraced by my Polish counterpart and her mother *Prababcia* as an integral part of the family—albeit twelve hundred miles away in another country. (See Chapter 2 for a more general account of Polish grandmothers.) What a surprise this was to me.
>
> When my son travelled to Poland to teach English, there was free movement for EU citizens and a feeling of real friendship and respect as young people explored the different cultures of the countries they arrived in. At the time, I was hosting students at my own house in the UK: French, Spanish, Polish, Chinese, Aussie, and Kiwi. As long as I had a good internet signal, they were all happy.
>
> When my son met a lovely woman, settled down and married in Poland, I began to see and experience the strong family ties of this wonderful matriarchal family. Prababcia (great-grandma) lost her husband and her son, her daughter Babcia (Maria) lost her husband too. And of course, they are surrounded by reminders of the Holocaust everywhere. So much sadness there, but much joy and strength too.

Along popped my two grandchildren, a boy and a girl. In my naivety I thought that I could learn Polish at the same time as they developed language skills. Very soon that idea was quashed as young brains sped way ahead of my dirge-like progress with this interesting language—my childlike testing of newly learned phrases from my phone app, such as *Dlugie Wlosy* (long hair) and *Krotkie Wlosy* (short hair), must have seemed like a command to my five-year-old granddaughter listening in the background because she promptly cut her long hair right there and then, well half of it. I must have been understood at least!

The internet has allowed my grandson to show me his important life moments in detail, such as an ear bud popping out of his ear hole in perfect time to the magic wand falling, clicking his fingers (advanced standard), and learning to whistle. Sharing stories is a delight as I have some of the same Roald Dahl books from my son's childhood and we can have real-time experiences turning pages at the same time twelve hundred miles apart. *Matilda* lives on. I have listened to violin and guitar practice, chuckled yet again in my life at Tintin and Asterix, listened to recitations of 'To be or not to be' at breakneck speed. It has been like opening a treasure chest of jewels I had no idea existed.

The tough bit is being older myself with a neurodegenerative condition, which means I have issues that are hard for others to understand, let alone young children. I am unable to bear raised noise levels (or even normal noise levels if hard floors are around), I have energy that runs out like an egg-timer, brain cut-off and brain fog. I try to reframe these in my mind. However, there is no arguing with fatigue and I can tend to be short-tempered and anxious if I am exposed to too much *joie de vivre* and boisterousness or more than one person talking at once.

I am sad not to be able to be there for the children in a way I would want to be. Prababcia, at the age of ninety-four, just takes herself off to bed after making a cake and I can learn from her. Polish Babcia has the gift of the most musical and infectious laughter and I can learn from her too. The warmth that exudes from these women towards young children has certainly been missing from my family background and I can learn from that as well. My daughter-in-law, intelligent and understanding, keeps me very much in the loop with videos and photos of bike riding, ice skating, school events, etc. The complete joy I get from watching these again and again is a tonic to the little world I now inhabit, and the pride I have in my son, watching his skill and patience while being thoroughly connected to his children and their emotional needs, is awe-inspiring.

I find myself having to be a very grown-up, distant, uncuddled sort of grandma, much the same as countless other mothers across the world as their offspring travel and settle down. All those grannies praying or wishing for the wellbeing of their families across the globe, that has to be a force for good.

Time, time, time …

Here's another tale of happy grannyhood from a grandmother who emphasises how important it is for her to be hands-on with her grandchildren.

Being a granny makes my heart glad. I feel such love for them, like I do for my kids, and, this time around, I have more time to give to them without the distraction of everything that goes along with being a parent, and it feels good to be able to indulge that, to not feel rushed to get them ready for anything, to indulge whatever they want to do, within reason. It doesn't matter if they 'help' to wash up and it takes ages and they get soaked, because I have time to do that with them. We can take a long time to walk from one place to another, we can sing songs, learn nursery rhymes, splash with a stick in water in the garden, toddle up and down the path for as long as it takes them to want to move on to the next thing, because we have the time. I think that's the most precious thing about being a granny for me, just having more time and space to enjoy each little moment together without having to rush to be anywhere else.

I feel really very fortunate to have a grandchild in a nearby town and another next door to me, so I can see one of them most days and the other (now at school) most weeks. To be so close and to have the kind of relationship that comes from that degree of familiarity is so precious to me. I try not to worry too much about the world they've been born into, but to give them as many positive experiences in small ways as I can. I concentrate on now and what I can give them that will stay with them.

Writing about being a granny has me looking at myself and what it is that I'm passing on to them. What makes me who I am, and on a simple level it's having fun together that seems important. We laugh a lot, and my just gone seven-year-old grandson has me in stitches with his stories and antics, and we laugh a lot together, and play, and make-believe and draw, and walk and play on the swing, and dance and tell stories. He loves telling me about his friends and the things he likes to do. He's kind and thoughtful, and serious about the skills he wants to develop, such as his dancing and drawing. He finds it hard sometimes when things don't work out right and is quite a perfectionist. He thrives on the attention I have the time to give him.

My little granddaughter at fifteen months is also full of fun and we love laughing together. She also loves to sing and dance and we do that together. She loves being outside, even in the coldest weather, and we walk to our field and feed the sheep (baa baas) every day and she loves to help throw them beets to eat. She squeals with delight, running around in her wellies. Being a granny is also, for me, about being able to help and support my children and their partners in a very hands-on way. I like that I have the opportunity to do this and that we're a big extended family.

When I was pregnant at twenty-two and I told my parents, I remember my mum being very clear about what she wouldn't be doing, and that was helping to look after the kids very much. She was pretty young herself at forty-five to be a granny (many grannies now are a lot older than this and can't run around having fun, much as they would love to) and she was reluctant to take on that role. We didn't live close by, but only a couple of hours away. When the children were old enough, she and my dad would have them for a week of the summer holidays and take them off in their campervan for a holiday, and my sister and husband would have them for a day of the week as well. That was the extent of help we had, which I was extremely grateful for, needing to work through the school holidays, and also it gave the kids some great memories of holidays with their grandparents, but in contrast I'm aware of how fortunate my own children are to have me living close by and being a very willing helper, eager to fulfil my granny role, unlike my mother. She even told me she didn't want to be called grandma but could my kids call her Persephone. She was actually only half joking (they were allowed to call her Gran). She loved them very dearly.

I feel like a proper cliché writing all this. They're such a huge part of my life and I cherish the times we have together. It can be tiring sometimes, but another cliché about being a grandparent is that at the end of the day you can give them back, put your feet up, and have a glass of wine.

She goes on to speak about another aspect of grandmothering in her life.

I have a different kind of relationship with my step-grand-children. The two oldest are now adults and when we see one another, which isn't often as we live a long way apart, it's great. We all get along well and enjoy our time together, but I didn't have the chance to be a close and constant support, or to be a big part of their lives when they were little. But when we did see them we had fun and now all have some very happy memories of time spent together, and they seem to value that time we had, as we do too. And then there's another one, a little girl, half-sister to these two, and I've only met her twice, so it's difficult to describe that relationship. I hope it'll develop in time.

The middle ones, who are now fourteen and twelve, haven't had a chance to develop a positive relationship with me or their grandad because of their parents' complicated separation and their perceptions of us having been coloured in a negative fashion (to put it mildly) by their father. We see them occasionally and support them all as much as we can, but it's not an easy situation, and being a granny to them hasn't been a happy or enjoyable experience for the most part, unfortunately. It's really sad and I wish it could have been different. I hope it can improve as they get older and they can form their own opinions.

I'm also step-granny to my son's stepson. Again, it's different. I didn't meet him until he was five and he already had strong relationships with his other grannies, so didn't see me as his granny and never has. I'm his little brother's granny and his step-dad's mum, not his granny. I look after him whenever I'm needed, along with his little brother, and we get on well, but I think my son and his partner would like it if I saw him and his brother in the same way. You can't force these things, it's different, and thus my response to how he behaves towards me. He can talk to me and we get on fine, but there's a distance which I don't feel with his little brother.

It is always, and perhaps inevitably, a complicated story. Here's another.

The importance of being grandma

This story charts the grandmother relationship over four generations.

'*Something about your experience with your own granny …*' I quickly dismissed this part of the brief when I was offered the chance to contribute to this collection of pieces about grandmothers. My own granny was someone quite outside my experience, both possible contenders having died by the time I was born. But I was certainly ready to share the magnificent and exquisite pleasures of being a grandmother myself. Or perhaps muse on the relationships between my mother and her six now-adult grandchildren, who all tell fond stories that keep alive the family image of 'grandma': a smartly presented, archly humorous matriarch, unerringly guided by her own common-sense morality.

Occasionally, she might be fazed by a bemused realisation that the rest of the world wasn't always following suit and in her final years—she died in May 2019, just short of her ninety-eighth birthday—she turned increasingly to her grandchildren to help interpret a world travelling in directions she could only hazily comprehend. An almost scornful, 'What does it mean, get the app?' was met with a clear and patient response from a grandchild who, like siblings and cousins, now eagerly uses the family WhatsApp group to mark grandma-related anniversaries, with real and virtual toasts recalling her fondness for a six o'clock gin most evenings.

When her first grandchild was born—my brother's child—my mother insisted on becoming 'Grandma'. 'Granny' she considered a rather insulting title, belittling of old ladies in general, whether grandmothers or not. 'Nanny' was too posh, implying a uniformed employee of the rich, or else, like 'Nan', 'Nana', or 'Gran', was deemed (by her) to be slightly common. [*The issue of names chosen and for what reason are explored in the Preface.*] None of this surprised me. I had observed and absorbed these views despite my un-grandmothered childhood, with friends and neighbours in our small rural town 'going up Nan's' for visits, asking 'our Gran; to make a birthday cake or having 'Granny coming to live with us'. I don't remember feeling envious or that I was missing out. If anything, several of these elderly women seemed to be at the centre of negative family dynamics that I might have been lucky to escape.

Not surprisingly, then, when my own children came along, my template for family living didn't include regular grandmothering. As we lived a hundred miles away from Grandma, this was just as well. My children were both over a week old when she travelled to meet them and, during their early years, it was generally we who visited her and my stepfather. I didn't really object to this. She organised Christmas, which I welcomed greatly, and at all times of year cooked lovely meals for us while we walked our children through beautiful countryside or visited friends nearby. To be fair, she did join us on some of these outings, but both my brother and I began to feel puzzled—and slightly peeved—that she never offered to babysit when either family visited her nor when staying in our own homes. She never considered having the children to stay without a parent and she rarely engaged with them in games or activities. Not once did she change a grand-child's nappy. Compared with many other grandparents in our social circle, she just wasn't interested in playing any hands-on role. She did knit for her grandchildren, enjoyed buying them books, and regularly performed a small repertoire of nonsense songs that held their interest, often at crucially helpful moments. But, by and large, her role was to offer dutifully practical support. There was also the occasional comment delivered from the sidelines, in the direct, no-nonsense manner of a Greek chorus. More than once, I was told I was making a rod for my own back.

Nevertheless, as the children grew, the watchful eye of the Greek chorus elicited increasingly curious comments. Right from the start, physical attributes and family resemblances had interested her. The varying periods of time between family get-togethers prompted her to remark on the children's changing appearances, personalities, and interests. Fortunately, the negative comments were generally kept for the parents' ears alone, and over time she turned with increasing pleasure and interest to the latest enthusiasms of articulate, older children, who became, as the years passed, stimulating young people whose company she enjoyed. They in turn became willing audiences for her stories and firmly held opinions, with scope for lively exchanges and differing views that did no damage to a broad mutual respect and, indeed, love.

It is difficult to say how or when Grandma was gradually elevated to the status of matriarchal icon. One factor was the admiration given to the unflagging energy she showed, in defiance of her years. Her skilful use of power naps led a grandchild to claim she had invented them. Her vitality was buoyed up by close attention to her grandchildren's aspirations and pride in their achievements. Pre-WhatsApp, she became the conduit for all family news, both significant and trivial. The grandchildren featured heavily here. She tracked all family movements around the globe, receiving cards and letters from various holiday destinations and longer trips, and readily reminded us all of each other's birthdays. Pre-Google, she was the go-to person for advice on stain removal or the perfect apple crumble and in return received help with setting up CD players or televisions.

Thinking around the question of her ever-increasing enjoyment in being grandma, I'm led to other thoughts about why my mother didn't embrace the role right from the start. Enjoying a reputation as something of a *raconteuse*, she was also adept at moving away from painful issues, wanting to avoid both her own pain and that of others. There was never a moment of huge revelation, but over many years and decades she divulged telling snippets and details of her life. Some of these had been deliberately hidden, as if shameful. Others that seemed to me quite significant were mentioned in passing, as if of little consequence. Our conversations around these topics might be prompted by looking at old family photos from her childhood—or, indeed, mine. Or they might arise through a crisis involving another family member. They were generally brief and quietly tentative on both sides, although I do remember one in which we both became bitterly loud and accusatory. Somehow, over time, there emerged some shared understanding of factors and circumstances that had contributed to my mother's ways of being. Facts and impressions came randomly to light, with no obvious sense of how they connected chronologically or otherwise, but I am now prompted to attempt piecing together some aspects of her life that seem relevant to her relationship with her grandchildren. [*As family work reveals, this is a vital clue to what happens in the now.*]

My mother was born in 1921, ten years after her brother and only sibling. Their parents had left a relatively poor rural community, a hundred miles away, for her father to take up more lucrative work. So, when my uncle and mother were born, there was no grandparental support on tap. Sadly, after each birth, my grandmother became ill. Whether this was purely physical or a form of postnatal depression, we don't know, but it does seem that the early mother–baby relationships were not straight-forward. My mother was told that her brother had 'lived with the lady from the sweetshop' for his first six months and that she too had spent time living with this neighbour for a brief period after her own birth.

However, throughout her childhood, my mother and her family spent many school holidays visiting both sets of grand-parents, who lived near each other in the countryside. They spent more time with the paternal grandparents who, in my mother's stories, certainly sounded more fun, especially her grandfather. My mother described her grandmother as 'always busy' with nine surviving children out of fifteen, my grandfather being the eldest. So, while clearly enjoying being around her when they visited, my mother didn't feel any particular bond with Grandma H. Even less emotionally accessible was Grandma M, large and formidable in photos and in my mother's memory. She was always well turned out and rather 'correct'. My mother had a vague sense that Grandma M was considered to be from a slightly 'better' class of family who felt that she had married beneath her.

When my mother was approaching sixteen, my grandfather retired and the family returned to their rural roots. Even in retrospect, she seemed unsure how she felt about this. She enjoyed the countryside but missed the dance hall, the cinema, the busy shopping centre and, of course, her friends. We spoke about this period of her life several times, and it came up again not long before she died, when she was at times confused, classically forgetful of recent events but often enjoying recalling the past. With some hesitancy, she described to me an abusive relationship she had experienced during the few months before she left the city. She had never told her parents about this and still felt some shame, although she also knew that what had occurred was not her fault. [*This is an important phrase to remember, echoing through all these stories: when there are difficulties, it's not necessarily your fault.*]

I've since wondered if this experience rocked my mother's self-confidence and played some part in a decision that we know she later regretted, which was to stop attending school. She enjoyed school and was doing well—I still have the school reports—and when the family were about to move, her teachers tried hard to persuade them all that she should transfer to a school where she could sit the School Certificate exams. The official story was always that her parents left the decision to her. They really didn't know any better and, anyway, she was keen to find work and earn money. But her heavily resigned regret that they didn't step in now makes me wonder if it disguised another, unexpressed regret and even anger, that her parents were ignorant of the abuse she experienced and too emotionally distant for her to turn to them for help. And, as I've said, perhaps her general confusion coloured her decision not to start at a new school.

Fast forward eight years. The Second World War is about to end. My mother has been married for a year, experienced an early miscarriage before realising she was pregnant but has now produced her first child, my brother. The family is living in the same rural area, in a small town that's a bus ride away from my grandparents' village. I'm not sure how the grandmothering role is shaping up, although there is clearly regular but not daily contact. Mother and baby seem to be doing well enough. My mother sometimes gets very agitated by the baby's regular crying but feels she must follow the four-hourly feeds prescribed by 'expert' Truby King. One day, when the baby is barely three months old, a neighbour of my grandparents arrives. My grandmother is very ill. My mother rushes to see her and on arrival finds she has died, aged fifty-eight.

The drama and shock of my grandmother's death was generally underplayed in favour of the next point in the story. Despite the obvious tension between her father and his son-in-law, my mother felt she now had to 'keep house' for her father. He wasn't particularly unwell or frail, but at the time it was the right and dutiful thing to do. She could see no alternative and the family moved in with him. One advantage was a bigger garden, with easier access for the pram to be wheeled out of close earshot. Fortunately, when I was born, a little over three years later, Truby King's advice was tempered by the winter weather and the discovery that being held on my grandfather's lap could sometimes stop me crying.

It seems that my parents had hoped their second child would arrive much earlier. Beginning to assume that my brother would be an only child, they started to negotiate taking over the running of the village shop but withdrew from this possible new venture when my mother became pregnant. She was always quite open with me that, at the time, she had mixed feelings. She had looked forward to working outside her home and, after I was born, the daily care of a baby and a young child, combined with the demands of her father, felt tough. The tension between my father and my grandfather was an added stress, spilling into my parents' relationship with each other. There were rows and accusations and, once, my mother even left home abruptly, staying away for several days. My brother and I were left with our grandfather, who had to break the news to our father on his return from work.

Details of this last event were first relayed to me during the final year of my mother's life. Neither my brother nor I have any recollection of it and were rather amazed, despite having been fully aware of her tenuous connection with babies and very young children. She had always speculated openly about how babies might develop as they grew older, keen for them to become bigger, stronger, less vulnerable, less needy and demanding. Perhaps she needed to defend against being in touch with her early feelings of neediness in relation to her mother and distant grandmothers. Her mother's sudden death so early in my brother's life must have disrupted her maternal focus on how best to respond to his needy screams and at the same time, perhaps, recognise some of her own unmet needs. That death also took away the possibility of the baby himself bringing about change, maybe creating greater warmth and closeness between mother and daughter. When speaking of family life after the move to her father's house, my mother's focus was not the absence of her mother, her baby's grandmother. It was more the struggle to make good her father's loss of companionship, to support his day-to-day living, alongside the conflicting needs of the rest of the family, including herself. She was trying, I think, to fill a void for him, which helped her to deny some emptiness and vulnerability of her own.

In order to focus on the aspects of her life that I have chosen to share in more detail, I'm now going to touch on some significant facts and events that were clearly powerful factors in my mother's whole story. They warrant more attention than I can give them here but they provide some ongoing background.

When I was around three years old, my grandfather died and we moved back to the small town. Once I had started school, my mother began to go out to work, as a bookkeeper, in an era when working mothers were relatively unusual. Life jogged along until, sixteen years after my brother's birth and her mother's death, my mother was suddenly and unexpectedly widowed. Two years later, she remarried. This relationship wasn't always easy, my stepfather's own painful family history coming into the mix. There were no step-siblings and his relationships with my brother and me were at first a struggle for all of us, but he always admired my mother and the marriage lasted until her death— more than fifty-six years—with my stepfather dying just three months later. For most of their marriage, my mother continued to work, right into her seventies and eighties when she went part-time.

The fallout from my grandmother's death resurfaced as my mother approached and passed the age at which her mother had died. The feeling that she might die at a similar age had always been around and was exacerbated when she received a cancer diagnosis that led to a hysterectomy. Shortly before the operation, my second child was born, a daughter. There are photographs of my mother looking down on the week-old baby in her arms. She is gently focused on her granddaughter but looks grey and sad—another new baby bringing echoes of past losses and perhaps heralding more to come.

However, my mother gradually recovered, while I became preoccupied with my family. She was clear that she wouldn't expect or accept any practical help from me at this time and I knew that she was well supported. I in turn accepted that her involvement with my children would be even more limited than if she were well, but I did experience some critical times when I might have been tempted to make demands and test her capacities as a grandmother. We spoke a lot on the phone and, as she recovered physically, her conversation became more animated. In relaying details of her post-op care and various appointments, she spoke warmly of a supportive, female GP who had picked up on some distress and created time and space for her patient to talk about how she was feeling. Dr J remained in post for many years and I'm sure she played an important part in helping my mother to find and sustain a new zest for life.

In the decades that followed, as her grandchildren grew, Grandma was in better shape to enjoy their company and admire their achievements. Their successes compensated somewhat for her own missed educational opportunities. Their interests fed her own and vice versa. There were discussions and questions about novels, films or television, outfits, past and future voting intentions, and places visited, complete with endless photos. As a more than competent pianist, she delighted in their musical achievements and ambitions. Her visits to our home became increasingly frequent, often built around attending a grandchild's concert or a trip to an exhibition or theatre. Grandma was willing to try new things and could sometimes surprise her grandchildren with her liking for some contemporary performance art or piece of sculpture. But in later years especially, she was more often scathing of newer works. The grandchildren then issued warnings of concerts likely to be 'not Grandma-friendly', a term still used to convey demanding contemporary content. Another phrase still in frequent use is, 'Grandma would love this', indicative of lavish period drama, romantic symphonies, or the sweeping grounds of an old stately home.

As well as following their education and careers, Grandma enjoyed keeping track of her grandchildren's love interests.

She met several potential long-term partners and rejoiced in those who eventually achieved this status. She took great interest in all six of them, who added to her dynasty and the stock of family stories with which to entertain and impress neighbours and friends. Three grandchildren married in her lifetime and at their weddings she was a much celebrated guest.

The grandchildren's partners also swelled the extended family's annual Boxing Day walk. Up to Grandma's final few years, this became an increasingly significant occasion, a country route followed by lunch at a family member's house. This was an opportunity for Grandma to draw admiration for her reputed energy and fitness and to engage in repartee with her willing audience. As the years passed, the day was increasingly centred around her house where as willing hostess, she enjoyed organising the menu and stage-managing the matriarchal show.

When space on the family stage was required for her first great-grandchild, rather than being threatened, Grandma's central position seemed enhanced. This new baby had elevated her to the rather gratifying status of Great-Grandma, a position firmly cemented by the ensuing arrivals of another eight babies. Of these, six were twins. This was not just any great-grandma, this was a great-grandma of three sets of twins and three singletons, the children and their parents all a source of wonder and praise, their very existence imbuing in her a sense of personal pride and achievement.

The new relationship gave rise to a new title, Granny-hop, a play on her name, partly intended to avoid confusion with a grandchild's in-laws. 'It makes me think of her hopping around,' the first great-grandchild told me. I was not surprised that, initially, Great-Grandma's responses to this were uncertain, but she warmed to the title, so that when the first of my own grand-children came along, that was how she signed herself to them. This, of course, left the way clear for me to start being Grandma. Not so long ago, I heard the broadcaster Esther Rantzen say, 'You love your children but you're *in love* with your grandchildren.' That rings true for me. My enjoyment of my grandchildren as babies was wonderful. I had been quite anxious as a new parent and, perhaps like my mother, keen for my own babies to grow into less vulnerable beings. With my grandchildren, two sets of confident and competent parents shouldered overall responsibility right from the start. I became a welcome and central part of a wider support network—important, but with time to watch and play or, like my mother, to cook and clean, so that the parents could enjoy time with their children. I was fortunate that, unlike my mother at the same stage of life, I was retired. I could spend unpressured time with them all and develop close, intimate relationships with each of them—not least during those nappy-changing processes that my mother somehow missed.

I became a grandmother seven years before my mother's death, at which point the ages of my five grandchildren ranged from almost seven to just over four years old. During these years, I was intensely and enjoyably involved with them all, but also began to spend increasingly frequent and lengthy periods with my mother, especially in her final year. One day she said, 'I wish I'd been able to talk to my mother like you and I talk. There are so many things I wonder about now.' I was at first surprised. I didn't carry a sense that she and I always talked openly, but on reflection appreciated that she had certainly become less guarded, wanting me to know facts, fears, regrets, and many other things before she died. I am grateful for this, but there are still 'things' that I too 'wonder about', including aspects of her childhood. They came to mind when I found in her house a present from my daughter. The foldable, reusable bag had a discreet inscription, 'Grandmas were once little girls'. This in turn reminded me of a photo, taken when my granddaughter was two months old and my mother ninety-one. She is turning to look down the four generational line of mothers and daughters, an expression of amused bewilderment on her face. How did I get from being a baby to here?

About six months after my mother's death, the family came together in her house. It was a positive day for us all and after the event, my brother referred to it as my 'first gathering as tribal matriarch'. This brought home to me the sense of a family void, a need to accept some aspects of the grandma role and a wish to enable further 'tribal gatherings', despite the challenge to my acknowledged skills. But the onset of Covid soon after this event has restricted opportunities for a full-scale get together, and sadly, as with so many families, Covid has also interrupted my relationships with my rapidly growing grandchildren.

However, for Christmas 2021, my daughter and family hosted my husband and myself. It was a small, low-key event in some ways, but full of emotions heightened not just by our limited contact in the previous two years but by a sense that Covid had halted our collective family adjustment to life without Grandma. My daughter has always loved Christmas and associated it with Grandma. Certain smells, carols, and Christmas decorations elicit a sigh of 'Ah! That reminds me of Grandma!' I have always felt that some of Grandma's talents have skipped a generation and my mother's competent granddaughter cooked a delicious traditional Christmas dinner. She used Grandma's recipes for apricot stuffing and bread sauce, serving the meal on long-familiar china from Grandma's house, her candle holder and candles on the table adding to the mix of celebration and acknowledged loss.

Not long ago, my son phoned. 'Normally,' he said, 'I'd have phoned Grandma with this question: can I use self-raising flour instead of plain in a crumble topping?' I found myself strangely flattered by his belief that I might be a satisfactory alternative to the hitherto preferred source. I was also touched by the reminder of a certain quality in their relationship, which he has come to miss. Perhaps too there was a slight challenge in the question—have I got what it takes to step up here? I hope I have but not in quite the same way.

On my fridge door is a card from my brother, sent shortly before our mother died. Two women smile at each other. The caption above reads, 'Sometimes I open my mouth and my mother comes out'. It echoes family assertions that I often sound like my mother. Even when she was alive, my son frequently commented, 'It's freaky! When you said that, you sounded just like Grandma!' My mother's stock response was an arch, 'Well she could do worse!' delivered in the style of Oscar Wilde's Lady Bracknell, implying a defence not just of speech and tone of voice but entire character and way of being. These days, I am the one to defend us both. 'I could do worse!' I say, just as archly. And I am conscious of the truth of this.

But I also feel that in some respects—and partly because of her—I've been fortunate to be doing just that bit better as well.

Supported and encouraged by my mother, I've had the benefits of higher education and consequently wider choices in life. The times into which I was born also supported this. I've been afforded opportunities to reflect on my relationships in ongoing ways that have held me together through times of crisis and, I believe, benefited my family, including, in later years, my mother. I wish she could have had more emotional support for herself, but I am grateful now for the richness of my relationships with my children and grandchildren, who make me value the importance and the huge pleasures of being Grandma.

Here above we have a rich and detailed account, which necessarily includes the idea of confidence in one's role, one's history of being grand-parented, and how these two interact with the modern grandmother who has to wrestle, successfully in many cases, with the mysteries as well as the vagaries of modern technology, apps, and the internet. Now, as one of my Italian commentators said, elderly grandmothers see the internet as a sort of modern fishing tackle. Woven in and out of these accounts are the developments of the twenty-first century and how grandmothers now grappled with them, or not.

Rich relationships develop over time. Below is the account of a granny, technically a step-granny, and her grandson who is now eighteen. They grow and thrive, basking in the safety of an attachment relationship (see the lecture on attachment on judithedwards.co.uk and C. M. Parkes' *The Price of Love*). Attachment is the relationship developed over time between parents, children, grandparents, and family. While loss and grief are inevitably a part of everyone's story, nothing worthwhile is completely lost but can be accessed in the mind, as my work with families over decades has shown. It can be 'lost' in the recesses of an individual mind, but can be 'found' again through reflection and talking. As Colin Murray Parkes observes, it is the price of love. This is the essence of psychoana-lytic and psychotherapeutic work. There may be resistances along the way, which can helpfully resurface in order for a smoother path to be achieved.

As a grandmother of an eighteen-year-old boy/young man, I have relished the privilege of having a great relationship with a growing and developing human being, without any of the day-to-day responsibilities of parenthood.

Although I am technically a step-granny, I've only ever been called Granny, which suits me. This role has been a special luxury for me, as I had no children of my own, so I bypassed the pleasures but also the pains and the ties of raising children. Instead I jumped straight into all the good bits of being a granny.

Like many twenty-first century families, our grandson doesn't have what used to be thought of as the standard quota of two grannies and two grandads. With both sets of grandparents having separated and found new partners, our grandson had eight grandparents when he was born. In fact, it was five grannies and three grandads, and one of the grannies was younger than his mum. More recently his own parents separated, and with his father having a new partner, he now has a further two (step) grandparents, so ten in total. Lucky boy! Well, maybe, but it can also result in complications, managed so far with grace by us all.

It's been a special treat to have had the relatively stress-free relationship with a growing young man without the need to be the one who has to remind him to do his homework, tidy his bedroom, treat women with respect, understand the importance of contraception, and the danger of drugs and excessive drinking. Taking for granted, but nevertheless grateful, that he has an ethical, anti-discriminatory, and caring approach to the world, thanks to his parents, leaving myself and my partner, his real grandad, to do the easy bits.

It's been a pleasure passing on books we've enjoyed and seeing them devoured from a young age. Not true of all books, of course. We were soon told that presents such as encyclopaedias and dictionaries were no longer necessary as he had all the information he needed on his smart phone. The upside of the tech-savvy younger generation, however, is that from the age of nine or ten onwards, our grandson has been the first port of call for problems when setting up new iPads, computers, and phones.

So yes, twenty-first-century 'Grandmotherland' is a good place to be. Hopefully, one to be enjoyed for another couple of decades or so, as my grandson blossoms yet further from boyhood and young man to adulthood and all the joys, and setbacks, the ups and downs—hopefully more ups than downs—that that will bring for him too.

Another story on the importance of being grandma looks at what can happen when your grandchildren are far away.

So, the best thing about being a granny … where to start? Maybe with a bit of background. My elder son has two boys, both of whom were born in Chicago. He and his ex-wife, the boys' mum, lived there for more than ten years. My first grandchild was also born in Chicago but was very premature and sadly lost his battle forty-five minutes into his short life. He would be nineteen now. Having grandkids so far away was incredibly difficult. I visited once a year and each time would have to re-establish the relationship. So tough not being around them to share their milestones: first step, first tooth, first words, etc. However, thank heavens for Skype. This at least meant we could see each other virtually on a regular basis and when we did see each other in person it wasn't as complete strangers. Thank goodness they came back to the UK after their mum and dad divorced and now live in London. [*Oh, how often this features in the story.*]

Being a granny is way more fun than being a parent. You don't have to make the rules and can even bend them to an extent. My favourite time with them as little ones was bath and bed time. There is something very special about reading a bedtime story to a clean, warm, sweet-smelling little boy. Night-time hugs and kisses and so much unconditional love. Now they are bigger (sixteen and eighteen) they have their own interests, but they never let me leave their house without a big hug, and all our phone calls and messages end with them saying, 'I love you so much.'

I still like to go and watch the younger one play football and the older run cross-country. It's even better doing this as a granny as you can choose which to go to. As a parent you have to go to every match and every race!

It is so much more relaxing being a granny, none of the hard stuff to do. You get to do all the fun stuff and hang out with them without having to be responsible for everything in their lives.

Best of all for me is seeing how my son has turned out to be a wonderful, caring father. He is a much better parent than I ever was.

The importance of humour

From New Zealand comes this story from a happy granny who can laugh at herself. It goes a bit like this.

> In my efforts to promote some sort of table manners and discourage eating almost everything with their fingers, I tried to encourage knife and fork as the preferred method of eating. On one occasion, a smarty child said to me, 'And Granny, what about Doritos? Should we eat those with a knife and fork?' In exasperation I said, 'Yes!' So they now tease me about telling them to eat Doritos with a knife and fork.

Humour is a great leveller—the ability to laugh at oneself is vital.

The comfort of grandma

Here are the memories from a Brazilian correspondent, who had the idea that Polish people found tenderness difficult—another cultural preconception.

> My maternal granny died when I was seven and I had little contact with her. However, I felt her to be very kind, though not tender. She was Polish and a bit mysterious. I was happy when she allowed me to explore her huge old house and also shared my playing with the only doll I ever had, which she had given me. Such a pretty doll it was, made out of porcelain, with a soft body, blue eyes like my granny and my mother. Actually she was more than pretty, she was beautiful. I can't recall how her porcelain legs got broken, but I put her on a high shelf in my wardrobe, stopped playing with her and never wanted another doll. Maybe this was when my maternal granny died. I don't remember. I refused to accept another doll throughout my childhood.
>
> My paternal granny died when I was forty-five years old. What I most remember from her as a child was her large, soft lap,

holding me and swinging me on her rocking chair. She dyed her hair black so carefully, and all her clothes were soft. I also have wonderful memories of the taste and smell of her cakes and cookies, specially prepared for her grandchildren.

What this shows us is that the attachment relationship includes soft comfort (being on Granny's lap) and smells which bring back memories long forgotten. Proust's memory of the Madeleine biscuit, representing the way in which tastes or smells can trigger long-forgotten memories, is repeated in small lives all over the world.

The questions that arise

This is another grandmother looking back, looking forward, being in the now.

> The experience of being a grandmother is not the same as being a mother. I was initially more hesitant and slightly nervous and getting to know my grandchildren took longer. But once the relationship was established it has been an enduring delight to learn about their experiences and watch them grow into adulthood. Now that most of them are grown up they amaze me with their knowledge of the technological world we live in, and they, in turn, are curious about the world I grew up in. We are mutually enriched as they look forward and I am asked, 'What was it like growing up in the last war, Grandma?'

Sometimes she is mean

In 'Speaking Up', the story below, it is the granddaughter who brings up a tricky subject about her mother. Will this threaten a previously good relationship?

> Holding my hand as I walked her home from nursery school, my four-year-old granddaughter looked up at me and said, 'Mum is mean sometimes.' 'Is she?' I asked, my heart stopping.
> I knew full well she spoke the truth, having occasionally witnessed this meanness in my daughter. But I felt gagged. I knew that whatever I said to my granddaughter on the subject would

be repeated to my daughter, which would be counterproductive. My daughter does not take criticism easily, most especially from me. Whether I talked to her via my granddaughter or spoke with her directly, I did not believe this would change her behaviour — except possibly to make the angry eruptions more frequent. I concluded that the only result of my saying something would be alienation. I would no longer be asked to walk my granddaughter home. [*This fear of alienation lies under the surface of most narratives about 'good grannies'.*]

It was a consolation knowing that my daughter is usually a wonderful mother, mostly fun and loving with both her girls. But the occasional outburst of meanness bothered me, especially because it was almost always directed at this granddaughter while her younger sister was coddled, babied, let off the hook.

I now regret saying nothing in the moment to my granddaughter and wonder what I should have said. I might have said, 'When this happens, you could just tell your mum she's being mean.' But to make her really realise this, you'd have to say it *only* when it is clearly true, not when she is just being a good mother in telling you not to do something for a good reason.

Last week I was finally able to speak about the problem with my older granddaughter, only now she is aged ten. I witnessed an instance when my daughter was again unfair to her eldest. When she left to do an errand with the younger sibling, I said, 'Your mum is sometimes mean. You probably don't remember, but you told me this when you were four.' I explained how I was bothered then and why I didn't think it would work to talk to her mother about the problem. Then I said, 'You know your mum adores you. Can you think of any reason she's harder on you than on your sister?' She thought about it and then shook her head. I said, 'It's simple. There's only one reason: you were born first. Remember this!'

The issue of why my daughter's frustrations erupt usually in relation to her older child is probably a little more complex, but I hit on the basic cause, when one child is privileged over another. It was such a relief to talk about it. I wondered if I couldn't have said the same thing to her when she was four. I knew my sensitive granddaughter would not relay what I said at age ten, but if she had repeated it at age four, would it truly have had such grave consequences? Perhaps the regret I carried about saying nothing for six years was worse.

However, one might also surmise that holding back had been less alienating, and had preserved the role of good granny, in the face of competing ideas and anxieties, which don't lie so very far beneath the surface.

Dealing with overwhelm

Good grannies often have a complicated role, as this story from a mindfulness teacher illustrates:

This story has a background, as any story has. My daughter, a single parent with four children, a son and triplet girls, started to live with a new partner. She conceives triplets again. She miscarries and loses two of the babies. One of the new triplets, her last daughter, survives. She is traumatised by these losses. My daughter is in overwhelm with the five children. The first four children are teenagers. Her new partner drinks too much and is a functioning alcoholic. I later find out that my daughter also has a drinking problem.

There is depression, a lot of chaos, parenting deficit and dysfunction in the house. One day, a row breaks out between my daughter and one of the triplets. My daughter cannot cope and verbally throws them out. A lot of hurtful things are said on both sides. My husband and I live nearby and are close to my daughter and all the grandchildren, supporting them as best we can. The girls are traumatised by the rupture and the perceived loss of love. Their father, who has remarried with two more daughters, is alerted and they stay with him in London. It is not feasible. They are all in education, pre their GCSEs and A levels, also are in a community with all their friends, in a country market town north-east of London. Their father's house is full and it is too far away for them to commute and to change schools. It is too complicated and not possible.

My husband and I decide to take them in. They come and live with us between the ages of fourteen and sixteen. Both my daughter and the children's father agree to this. Child benefit is routed our way to help financially. They see their father most weekends and have no contact with their mother. Both me and my husband are working as therapists and in our sixties. We don't have a large house, but we do live within walking distance of the girls' school. We buy a single fold-up bed, extra towels, etc. and the girls take our bedroom, with one on the new fold-up bed and the other two in our bed. We move to the sofa-bed downstairs, daily opening it out and folding it away. The girls are understandably traumatised, angry, and confused, and yet there is a resilience from having each other and they are very happy to be with us.

Going from the two of us, suddenly shopping and washing and cooking for five and seeing clients was a new demand energy wise. Two of the girls continued their paper rounds, which were not so close by now. We had some very early mornings either taking them or picking them up when the weather was really bad. They loved that they were welcomed home after school, had regular meals, a clean and tidy home, and could curl up on the sofa watching films, talking through relationships with girlfriends, walks, playing games, and even the discipline of having to do their homework. When they had finished schooling and the time came for them to leave, they rejoined their father, who moved closer. I missed them so much, a full-on 'empty nest' syndrome. But it was also wonderful for my husband and I to have our bed and our lives back as an ageing couple. They still come occasionally and have a sleepover, which is joyous for us all.

As to my own history, I am an only child and my mother was an only child. My daughter has broken the mould by having five children, including a son. My parents met in Australia. My mother came from a background of Scottish émigrés and my father was in the Merchant Navy. There is mystery around my mother's birth and background. I never met my maternal grandmother and my mother never spoke of her parents or background. My father mentioned her as a Scottish woman with the sixth sense. I never knew my maternal grandfather's name. My parents divorced in England when I was about four years old after my father left my mother for another woman, his second wife.

My paternal grandmother, being one of eight children, had many grandchildren. I was from my father's first of three marriages and grew up with my mother. My grandmother was somewhat remote yet kind to me when I saw her very occasionally. I always felt an outsider, being a child from my father's former marriage. Irish, born in the Argentine, this grandmother was very respected in the family and taught Spanish into her eighties. My grandfather had been an engineer, made and lost fortunes. My grandmother trailed around various parts of the world with an ever-increasing brood of children. One of her children, my aunt, persuaded my grandmother eventually to leave her husband. There were goings-on in the family that were not okay, but I won't talk about them here. At any event, it's a complicated tangle.

My first marriage fell apart while I was living abroad. I returned to England. Upon my return, my mother and my grandmother died a month apart, when my daughter was three. Such loss for us all.

I single parented my daughter from the age of two until she left home when she was eighteen. I didn't have the experience of parenting alongside a father or partner or having any family support. So, when the triplets came to live with my husband and myself (I had married again, later), it was as though life had given me the opportunity to experience parenting again, with the support of a deeply kind, loving man willing to partake in the healing of my family. It was a wonderful gift. This gave the girls the feeling of being held by a loving family. My husband had three boys from a previous marriage. He had no experience of teenage girls!

I kept working as a craniosacral therapist. I was sixty-four. When I was bringing up my daughter, I struggled financially, with ME (chronic fatigue syndrome), loss, aloneness, and depression. Eventually I had several years of psychotherapy to help me unravel my complex upbringing. My parents had divorced when I was around four and my mother, who was deeply troubled and secretive, died of anorexia complications. I gradually became deeply compassionate towards my mother's background and struggles. My father, as I said, had remarried: a woman who did not welcome me in. I carried a lot of guilt and shame at not being able to offer my daughter a secure, stable family upbringing. With no clear role model, my parenting skills were sketchy, yet I always had a lot of love to give and had some wonderful friends. Animals and nature were my saviour.

When the girls arrived to live with us, my heart swelled. It was full on, but I was blessed with a meditation and yoga practice which I fitted in as best I could. I had a ground and a quieter place within that I did not have when bringing up my daughter. I had not disciplined my daughter. I was a child of the Sixties when the culture was to be free and rather lacking in boundaries. Dr Spock, so benign in many new ways, influenced us to let our children cry. (This still pains me to remember that I did this.) With the girls I found a balance within the joy of being with them and a clear place when behaviours were 'not okay'. They knew by the tone of my voice and my words that they had overstepped a boundary. No isolating them on a naughty step!

My dear husband was wonderful with them and also challenged by hormonal female teenagers. Through the challenges we all became closer and closer. There was a lot of humour, banter and teasing, snuggling on the sofa together, watching films, playing games, alongside a lot of explosions and teenage moods. We are all very tactile so there was a lot of hugging and gentle holding. Born minutes apart, the girls each had their own unique expression towards their mother, and their anger and rage at what had happened and was still happening. Each manifested the rupture in their own way: one with grief and the terror of abandonment, one with anger, rage and defiance, and one with insecurity and demands for attention. It felt very important to offer them the space for their feelings, where they were free to talk about what was happening for them. At times I was in contact and talking with my daughter. She was grateful that we had taken them in, and also full of confusion, anger, blame, denial, guilt, and shame. As a mother and a grandmother my heart needed to be open and as free as possible of judgement of all of them. It was deeply saddening to be caught in the middle of their pain and all these emotions. I had times of tipping into self-blame, going over in my mind the 'what had I done so wrong?', recapitulating this line of ruptured disconnect through the mother line in my family.

Forgiveness perhaps will come gradually with time and with more understanding and individuation. The balance, with the girls, came with the joy of being with them, being free to express my unconditional love, their innate loving and humour, and, in my heart, my commitment to healing this ancestral line of women and grandmothers to be. We had the usual teenage behaviours to manage, such as their moods, fighting among themselves, boyfriends, friends, drinking, smoking, parties. We came to know and be fond of some of their friends who were very supportive of the girls. Overall, they were so alive and vibrant, and we had and have a deep love and respect between us all. To our joy they all survived their A levels and did well.

Their elder brother was left at home with his mother, her partner and the youngest sister. He was my first grandchild and my first deep love as a grandmother. Also, my first challenge for grandparenting. He was born abroad in Germany where my daughter lived with her first husband who was in the army. The first night we stayed with them I woke in the night to hear my grandson crying. They did not get up to soothe him. I was distraught but knew I could not interfere. My daughter's husband was not sympathetic to his son's crying. Finding the right boundary as a grandparent can be very tricky. I learned to take advantage of the spaces and places where it was possible to share this unconditional love with my grandson. The youngest granddaughter is very close to her father and his family and so we don't have so much connection.

A couple of years later, I woke very early one morning and went downstairs into the kitchen. My mobile rang at 5 a.m. It was my daughter. She had hit rock bottom and was drinking an inordinate amount of vodka. It was the first time she had owned her drinking problem. She had frightened herself. A veil was being removed and she was exposed to herself and all the pain. We spoke for three hours and to my relief she agreed to see the doctor. My husband was wonderfully wise and supportive. We were early for the doctor and sitting in the car park, I asked her how long she had been drinking like this. She then told me (I had not known before) that she had been raped when she was fifteen and it started then, thirty years ago. While I knew she had a problem, I had not fully understood or been able to comprehend how much and for how long.

A lot of understanding of all the past troubles began to fall in place. With luck she saw a wonderful doctor who asked just the right questions, listened, and was kind. I sat next to her in the surgery, quietly shaking. It took her so much courage and I felt immensely proud of her amidst my fears for her health and wellbeing. My daughter had an alcohol-related rash on her skin, so we drove to the market square for a prescription. My daughter remained in the car. When I came out of the chemist shop, much to my amazement I heard bagpipes. A street musician was playing. I had never heard them before, or since, in our town. Deep, deep tears welled and I felt that our Scottish ancestors, the line of mothers and grandmothers, were with my daughter. The music rose through time bearing the gifts of the wise. I got into the car and shared this with my daughter and together we wept and held each other in the embrace of this force of ancestral love, care, and pain.

Some years later, with the triplets, who were full of a confusion of love, anger, and hatred towards their mother, I felt a need to try to bring them together with their mother in some way. I proposed a meeting. They agreed and I invited my daughter to sit with them round the kitchen table. I had a talking stick. I suggested that this was just a beginning to open communication. We would just have an hour. The rules were to talk with the stick and then to listen and not talk over each other. I would hold them to that but not speak into the circle. I had no idea how this would go but was encouraged by the fact that each of them was willing to turn up. Each spoke, in their own way, of how it felt for them and then, with enormous courage, my daughter told her story. There were lots of tears. This was the beginning of slowly healing the rift. I was so proud of all of them. That was some years ago now and my daughter has not had a drop of alcohol since. They still struggle with their mother and her partner and her way of life. The girls, with strong work ethics, are making their way in the world, determined to have a better life for themselves.

A good granny indeed, who stepped up to the plate in a way which is so admirable, given her own shaky start in life. Her mindfulness training has indeed served her well, as she can record, recall, and observe both how things were stuck and how they changed over time. Time is indeed the essence of work here, done either with a therapist or not, and instant change is a fantasy, though one that may be wished for. 'Mild amelioration' may be a more realistic aim than a 'cure'.

Healing with feeling

Here to end this chapter is the account of a good granny to be reckoned with. This robust woman telling her story is a psychotherapist, buttressed by her conviction that speaking about feelings is an important route towards healing them. This is 'passion' in action. It contrasts with the feelings that may be held in, suppressed, and eventually burst out. Over the years I have observed with interest that children whose feelings have not been attended to can burst out, as they betray their interest in volcanoes, volcanic eruptions, and loud fireworks. As my contributor declares, 'Don't mess with this nana!'

I was delighted when I first learned I was to become a grandmother but a little afraid I wouldn't feel anything when the baby arrived. I cannot overemphasise the love that overwhelmed me when I saw, heard, and spoke to my first grandchild or the three that were to follow over the next six years.

An experience of picking one of my grandchildren up from school, when she was in reception, illustrates the life and passion infused in me by my role as Nana, as they all call me. Alice came out in a line of other children to be collected by their 'grown-up' from the playground. Her face was glum and her eyes dark as she fixed me with an intense stare. There was no sign of her usual exuberance where she would be skipping along chatting to her friends. I noticed that two of her friends had cheap plastic toys that they were flashing at their grown-ups with smiles of delight. Alice ran towards me and fell into my arms. Crying her eyes out she told me that she hadn't got a go in the dippy box, the weekly reward for meeting some requirement imposed by the teaching staff. I was filled with feeling and wanted to go and give the teacher a piece of my mind. Instead I spoke to Alice loudly enough for the teacher to hear. I said, 'I know it doesn't help with how hurt and disappointed you are feeling at the moment but you are a beautiful, intelligent girl and your time in the dippy box will come.' I shot the teacher my own dark stare as I passed. Don't mess with this nana!

CHAPTER 4

Finding your place

In which we consider the lives of those who are not grandmothers: a great sorrow or a great relief?

Some women choose not to have children (or can't have them, which is a very painful thing to have to mourn, not to be taken lightly by anybody) and this chapter tells a few stories about how these women adapt to find a place in the world as they age.

That word 'sterile', often used of a woman who can't have children, has multifaceted meanings. The women in this chapter, who have chosen for one reason or another not to transmit their genes, are creative in so many other ways, through painting, through teaching, through yoga, through finding a way to be themselves rather than adopt a mask. Downward-facing dog this is *not*. As eighteen-year-old soldier Alexander Ruika, an apprentice in the Stasi Regiment, wrote, 'Away with the masks ... admit you are yourself, and your neighbour too.'

One of my contacts told me, 'When you feel lucky to be alive, as I do, then childlessness comes way down the list of what troubles you. But people won't hear that. They have a narrative pre-prepared, and it doesn't fit. I want to insist, women are not only agents of transmission.' Indeed. It was Martin Luther who said, 'We should not mourn if our wives or daughters die in childbirth—they were only doing what God made them for.' Time moves on—women's creativity is hailed now as being equal to that of their male counterparts in the human chain, and here below are a few stories to illustrate this, where the absence of 'the pram in the hall' has caused the blossoming of other talents.

The artist's story

I have never regretted nor missed not being a Mother (with a capital M). I certainly would not have wanted to become one like my own mother.

The time was never right and I often thought, seeing so many difficulties that can develop with children and parents over time (see Chapter 6), that I was not deprived. Very rarely, many years ago when visiting friends who had recently had a child, I might experience a mild sense of loss, but it never lasted. And to lose the bond of love and affection you may once have had as either a child or a parent, by growing apart, would, I felt, be painful.

As a painter it meant that had I also been a mother, the role of both or either could have suffered or been compromised by demands made on each and time would have been difficult to divide. I do have the advantage of being an aunt and a great aunt, 'Grauntie Mim', as my nephew named me, and I am also a step-grandmother. My relationships with all nine of my nieces and nephews, great and small, and with my step-grandson are very good, so I have no feeling of deprivation. When my Italian grandson was born his mother suggested I be called 'Nonna Mim', but I always wanted to be called just by my name, Mim (despite spellcheck often trying to make me into a Mum), and I resisted the title, though I am rather fond of Grauntie, as great-aunt.

My dear partner and later husband, when I asked him at the outset how he would feel if I became pregnant, replied, 'I would tell you, no, ask you, to keep it.' But it never happened and I think our great relationship over thirty-six years, and with our respective creative careers, benefited from not having had children. But of course there was always the underlying security of knowing that if I ever did become pregnant, our child would have been wanted. So I have never felt in any way incomplete, but perhaps enjoyed more the freedom and independent choices my lifestyle brought being a non-parent.

The educator's story

To be a good grandparent you have to like the grandchildren. Our mother didn't like us much and was full of complaints about our behaviour and appearance. She was the same about my sister's children, although the evidence that she loved them was that she sent large sums of money for them. My sister got as far away as she could and lives in the USA. She brought her children home in hopes of fostering a relationship with their grandmother, but it was never a success.

Our mother hadn't been well mothered as she lost her mum when she was tiny, spent some years in an orphanage, and then lived with her father and a stepmother. I think she envied our childhood as it was more comfortable than hers and we didn't, of course, know that and weren't grateful. Also, maybe she hadn't experienced the joy that children can bring so didn't seek to find it.

So because I didn't learn about emotional parenting or taking joy in children, I didn't crave them like some of my friends did. In the Sixties, I had a friend who wanted a baby so much she had one without being married. I just couldn't understand that.

I like children and that's why I became an educator. I have given a lot of my life to trying to get for children what they should have. I was never desperate to be a mother and I guess that's because I didn't know it could be satisfying and because I knew I was still a child inside.

When I was married and pregnant, I put off ringing my mother to tell her for so long that in the end my husband did it. I was afraid to tell her, though unsure why. Perhaps I was afraid of her envy, or of her attempt to take control somehow. I subsequently had a miscarriage and life moved me on. I chose to do something else, to be distracted from the pain.

I have known two or three women who had children without being married and didn't tell the father there was a baby, and one single father who knew but didn't tell his parents. So many grandparents never know. I think that may be an attempt by parents to keep all the power, which of course they have anyway.

I only knew my grandfathers briefly. I remember one enjoyed being with me and the other one consoled me when my parents were cross. That's because we lived in the same house and so he knew every situation. Now families don't live together, that sort of understanding and comfort is harder to offer. But the reverse can be true and living close by may indeed be 'too close for comfort'.

I do think back down the years to my grandmothers, though. My paternal grandmother died when my father was about twelve. The story is that she kept complaining of toothache and they took out all her teeth in the end but she still had toothache. She finally died in hospital of that kind of pneumonia you get from lying down too much. I can just imagine a woman dominated by a quick-tempered, obstinate husband who might clench her teeth endlessly, and I feel sympathy for her. She couldn't win her power game and that is a feminist issue.

I didn't have a particularly happy childhood and I read fiction non-stop to get myself to a more comfortable place. I remember as a teenager I was allowed to go out to see my friends at church on Sunday nights. I used to spend too long doing schoolwork all Sunday and leave getting ready for church until it was very late and I was in danger of missing the bus. Looking back I can see that ensuring I was working or rushing was a protection from unhappiness and the fear of stress at home.

During my late thirties and early forties, intellectually I wanted a child and knew I would regret it later if I didn't have one. Also I was aware that I didn't have much time left. But emotionally I was somewhere else. I was the head of a school, spent my days with children, and always had a reason why the work would suffer if I stopped for pregnancy leave, so I just let the situation run on. I was divorced by then and I never really had faced all the failure of that. If I had stopped working every waking hour, the pain and regret would have swamped me. So I just carried on working. It was only years after retirement, when I had time and strength to reflect, that I realised what I had been doing all my working life.

Now I'm at an age where my friends are grandmothers and I no longer have the distraction of work. I fill my time with 'imitation work'. I deal with people who need help at a local charity and I play a strategic role as a school governor, trying to do it right for the children. That keeps me stable and needed, but

I am still aware that in the future I may have to relinquish those occupations so that life will be empty. Also, I won't have many people to care for me.

I see children and grandchildren belonging to my second husband and to my sister. I feel a bit like my mother felt—I'm not close to them and don't care for them much. I entertain them and talk with them but I don't seek them out.

I know I am missing that thread of continuity that families have. A relative told me that grandparents take comfort in old age from knowing the young in the family will repeat patterns and experiences that the grandparents have had, and will improve on the learning and living, so that part of the grandparents goes on. I know that I can look to my sister's family for that and that there will be something there for me, although not as much as there would be if I had my own children.

My sister's daughter divorced when one of her children was only three. My sister, his grandmother, gave the child breakfast, dressed him, took him to school on her way to work, picked him up from school after work, fed him, and got him into his pyjamas for his mother to collect. She did that every week night for many years. That was Milton: I thought he would turn out to be a disaster but he is a very successful teenager now, well mannered, polite, good with his younger cousins. My sister and her husband gave him what he needed at some personal cost, but it was worth it.

What we see here is acute pain being masked by distraction and an underlying wish that is never fulfilled. Here is a woman who has given a great amount of her life to helping children, hugely valuable work, and does now what she calls rather dismissively 'imitation work'. But as she says early in this account, 'I knew I was still a child inside.' The intergenerational story has an effect on current history, as the woman's own mother had not been surrounded by a mother's love, and there remains a sadness which underlies this particular story. So, are we thinking about a great sorrow or a great relief? In many senses these two concepts are intertwined. Is the great relief a defence against feeling sorrow, or is there relief to be obtained when one is not assailed—even attacked—by the prevailing norm?

The queer woman's story

I don't have children, I didn't want them and don't want them. I say this as I stride out the other side of menopause. It wasn't a strategic decision, or even a decision at all, the idea simply did not occur to me.

Of course, I've considered the question, from a meta position, because I am female and have occasionally been asked. But, for the most part, I may as well have been asked, 'Do you want to grow gills?' since that was equally as relevant in my view or, in other words, not at all.

I've never had to 'defend' my position either because it was assumed by many that because I am queer I would not want to have children, could not for practical reasons, or should not for skewed moral reasons. That's suited me since it has meant that I haven't been bombarded with expectation, unlike many of my straight female friends.

So at fifty, having been asked by a dear friend if I'd write about not having children, I am truly trying to think about it in depth for the first time. But it remains hard for me to get past gills. I don't even want pets. I've had pets, and really like cats and dogs, also rats, chickens, horses, goats, and donkeys. But since our last cat died, the relief I feel at not having to worry about her when we are away is a heavy weight lifted. Now we have no pets, or animals of any sort, or children. We have suitcases and travel a lot.

My wife and I were in our forties when we met. She didn't have any children from her previous marriage and says no more on the subject than she wasn't interested in having children. She's American and I'm British.

I'm still stuck at gills. Do other women really get possessed by the urge to have children? Do men? Or is it mainly just an outcome of an often enjoyable activity loaded with expectation from the world around? Did I choose not to have children or did they all choose to have children? I asked my mother once if she'd have all of us again—five of us born between 1952 and 1969. She replied that while she loves us all deeply, she might choose, if presented with life over again, not to have any children but instead to take lots of lovers and have a career. I flinched at the idea of my mother having lots of lovers and didn't press any further, turning away instead as she qualified, 'Your dad was good at it, you know ...' My mother is an Irish Catholic, didn't use birth control and apparently enjoyed my father at least five times. She didn't choose to have children and wasn't aware that she might choose not to, being a woman at a time when birth control was trickier. Even with the news that she was pregnant with me in her forties, desperately depressed at the prospect of another child, she didn't choose to have an abortion. She considered it, she told me, but her faith denied her that choice.

Maybe I'm the quirk and am simply devoid of maternal drive. I know that for some women not being able to have children is deeply distressing, for others that decided not to there may be years of regret. And I don't mean to make light of that. But I'm very happy not to have children. Or pets. It has meant I have lived much of my life on a curious whim. I've been a London bus driver, bus mechanic, landscape gardener, artist, and business consultant, to name a few. I founded and ran an advertising and design agency in London for a decade. I have also lived and worked in Toronto, San Francisco, and Washington, DC. These days I live with my wife at Wrightsville Beach in North Carolina and donate much of my time to local non-profits, when not attending to our business. We can both jump on a plane to the UK and see our family and friends there without too much fuss or preparation. This is also helped by not having the expense of children, which I might add is much more in the US than the UK if your hope is for your child to go to university.

However, I haven't been without young people in my life. I have eight nieces and nephews, nine great-nieces and -nephews, and my wife has a niece and a nephew. I've enjoyed watching the youngsters of my family grow up and become parents themselves. Seeing their youthfulness finally solidify into something belonging to the past, as they ease into the ongoing responsibility of parenthood. It's rather beautiful to watch. But the prospect when considered in the context of me remains: gills.

I suppose if I'd had a child, he or she would be twenty or even thirty by now. How weird would that be, to have issued another human that's now an adult and carrying half of my genetic material. I wonder who the father would have been and what the child would have been called. Actually, I don't wonder those things. If I think about it, I feel a degree of claustrophobia followed by immediate relief as soon as I bring myself back to the reality that I don't have children.

I'm very happy that I end with me and, when I'm gone, that's it. Is there a phobia of passing on your own genetic material? I mean, I happen to think I'm quite decent and rather funny (my wife doesn't entirely agree with the latter), but I don't like the thought of continuing on via another now that I am brought to thinking about children, my children.

So as I age and my uterus packs up and leaves, I sit on the porch with my wife, a glass of wine in hand, and we discuss our next trip back to the UK and why we can't keep lavender alive in a pot. Perhaps ask me when I am seventy. I doubt I will feel any different, but I may want a pet again by then.

The yoga teacher's story

I posed a few questions to a woman who chose not to have children.

Did you ever feel the desire for kids?
Yes, I did. I must have been in my thirties and after having an abortion and an ectopic pregnancy, I was curious to know if I could have a child, but it was only curiosity, not a strong desire to have a child.

When and why did you decide against it?
I think I knew all along that motherhood was not for me. I never had a feeling that it was important for me to be a mother. Since arriving in the UK at nineteen, I have felt very independent and I much like my sense of freedom.

Have you regretted it?
No!

What has replaced them if they need replacing?
To be honest, I do not see the need to replace children with anything. I live a fulfilled life, like my own company, like what I

do, and travel. I also have a good relationship with my partner who does not want children either. However, I do like children, someone else's children, I can see that they bring freshness to life, but after a couple of hours I feel that I have had enough and want to give them back to their parents and go back to my own person, freedom, time, silence.

The stories in this chapter serve to show us that some people, even those doing what they dismissively call 'imitation work', live happy and fulfilled lives without feeling they have to conform to some sort of prescribed 'norm' when it comes to having children.

As the yoga teacher said, 'I do not see the need to replace children with anything.'

CHAPTER 5

Little Red Riding Hood: a granny story

In which we stop off at a library ...

Tales morph over time. I asked many people which story about a grandmother came instantly to mind and it was usually Red Riding Hood and her visit to her granny. Possibly she is the most iconic grandmother from folklore—and would you believe it, there are fifty-eight versions of this time-honoured tale. It's a story told in different ways around the world. Most of the people I asked came up with this one (including the Chinese version mentioned in Chapter 2 and told in full in this chapter). Why was this the story people chose? Little Red Riding Hood goes to visit her grandmother, only to discover that a wolf has eaten the old lady, dressed in her clothes, and now plans to eat the little girl too. In terms of our theme about grandmothers, what can we deduce here? I hope the reader will forgive me for trying to delve beneath the surface to puzzle out other ways of seeing this iconic tale, apart from the obvious one. This again is what therapists do, digging beneath the surface of 'the obvious' to what may lie partially or completely buried underneath.

What happens next depends on which version you hear. Was Little Red Riding Hood devoured? Did a passing huntsman cut her from the wolf's belly? Did she trick the wolf into letting her go outside? In parts of Iran, the child in peril is a boy because little girls wouldn't wander out on their own. In Africa, the villain could be a fox or a hyena. In East Asia, the predator is more likely to be a big cat.

This chapter looks at just one archetypal story. There are the bare bones of the story, what may lie underneath, and what may still lie underneath the underneath.

Stories are storehouses containing the deepest truths about human desire, conflict, self-deception, as we find ourselves reflected in the characters. Archetypes of the mother and the grandmother are some of the most sacred in all cultures. Life of course would not exist without mothers and, in myths and legends across the world, there are also powerful grandmother figures. These older women represent the crone aspect of womanhood, connected to ageing, dying, nature, and the powers of the underworld. This theme, then, links up with women as witches, but that is beyond my remit here. These women are caring, wise, supportive, and powerful matriarchs, who heal the sick but yet may come to be distrusted because of their 'magical' powers to aid people in becoming better.

A Roman tale

So where shall we start? We could look at the Roman altar on Via Flavia, near modern-day Fiumicino airport, which was found after excavations at the end of World War Two. It's about a woman saluted both as grandmother (*avia*) and as wet-nurse (*nutrix*). Her name was Claudia Berus and it was set up by her grateful grandchildren, Claudius and Claudia. Maybe she was wet-nurse when their mother died. At that time grandmothers were still young enough to have milk in their breasts. What story would she tell if she could, we can wonder. In any event, her two grandchildren loved her deeply, deeply enough to erect a monument which can still be read today.

The theme of a grandmother offering her breasts for feeding is attested to in medieval tales, often connected with situations of poverty and crisis: the mother died and the grandmother had searched in vain for a wet-nurse. Sometimes, the theme of the *Virgo Lactans* (the lactating Virgin) is added to strengthen the miraculous character of the report. Although at first sight the phenomenon seems strange and utterly impossible from a medical point of view, anthropological research in both Africa and Oceania has attested to very similar facts.

Up to old age, women (quite often the grandmothers) continued to offer breastfeeding. They either performed the tasks of wet-nurse over an extended period of time or they returned to the task of offering milk by drinking portions of coconut milk and having their nipples stimulated by suckling infants.

Here's to the old hag!

Let's now leave ancient Rome and travel along the shelves to medieval Finland.

In the old Finnish language, *akka* was an honorary term given to any elderly woman. There are areas in northern Finland where words *akka* and *akku* mean grandmother, but in modern Finnish *akka* mainly means an old hag. What happened here? This is something we can ponder, linking it up with both the classic story of Little Red Riding Hood and the one recounted by my Chinese correspondent later in this chapter.

The story of Akka began seven thousand years ago when the Baltic tribes arrived in southern Finland, bringing their gods and goddesses along with them, as was customary and as we still do. The character of Akka is partly based on the Lithuanian earth goddess Madderakka of the Saamis. Very little is known about Finnish Akka. She goes by many names: Maannakka, Maanutar, Manteretar. All these names are derived from the word *maa*, meaning earth. *Akka mantereenalanen* is a common title used in spells and it means 'the woman who lives beneath the earth'. Akka was the goddess of earth, soil, and vegetation. She was the creator of snakes and worms (*mato*). It was believed that during *matopäivä* (the day of the snakes, what we call the spring equinox), Akka woke up after the long cold winter and all the snakes woke up from their hibernation, dancing in her honour. Worship of snakes was very common in ancient Finland and in all Baltic countries. And this of course links up with our theme about women as witches, feared for the very powers from the earth they use to heal.

It is thought, though not proven, that the cult of Akka was destroyed in the early Middle Ages when Christianity arrived in Finland. For a long time, Catholicism and pagan customs were practised alongside one another, as they were in many parts of the world, including Great Britain. Akka morphed into the Virgin Mary, the giver of all life. At the same time, her image changed from a wise woman into that of an old evil hag. So take note when we reflect on our principal story, of Little Red Riding Hood. Something similar happened to Louhi, the Finnish goddess of the moon and shamanism. She was downgraded to become the goddess of death and the underworld. In many myths, the roles of Akka and Louhi are intertwined and it becomes tricky to disentangle them.

Roots, routes, and branches: some theories about the origins of the story

Where did the original story of Little Red Riding Hood come from? Scholars have been puzzling over that for years. Jamie Tehrani, an anthropologist at Durham University in the United Kingdom, thinks he's found the answer. He believes that folk tales, like biological species, are handed down but with slight alterations along the way.

In many ways, the problem of reconstructing folklore tradition is very similar to the problem of reconstructing the evolutionary relationship of species. We have little evidence about the evolution of species because the fossil record is so patchy. Similarly, folk tales are only very occasionally written down—they are handed down orally and it is the powerful ones that survive.

Tehrani used a methodology called phylogenetics. Oh how wide your roots are spread, Red Riding Hood, exclaims the author of this book, wider and more extensively resonating than your 'grand-mother's' ears!

You reconstruct history by inferring the past that has been preserved through inheritance (as we argue with the granny meme, the idea of 'The Granny' which can become stuck and ossified). The descendants of ancestral species will resemble them in certain ways. You can figure out which features of a related group of organisms or folk tales could be traced back to a common ancestor. Is the common ancestor here the wolf? The other side of the benign granny—oh Granny Wolf, what deep roots you have in the universal unconscious …

It's been suggested (in error) that the tale was an invention of Charles Perrault, who wrote it down in the seventeenth century. Other people have insisted that it has far more ancient origins and now we know that this is true, as well as having the support of Tehrani in our thinking. There's an eleventh-century poem from Belgium which was recorded by a priest, who says, 'There's this tale told by the local peasants about a girl wearing a red baptism tunic who wanders off and encounters this wolf.'

Here he/she is again. No wonder it was the first tale people recalled. It's deep in our very cells … 'Lift the latch, my darling, and walk in …' Our unconscious thinking holds keys to many thoughts we didn't know we had.

Various versions and central themes of Little Red Riding Hood

Here's a story from China, told by my Chinese correspondent, rewritten by me, continued from Chapter 2.

In the early Jin Dynasty (1115 to 1234), there was a family with a father, mother, and three children. The father went to join the army and the mother made and sold clothes in the market. One day, the mother went to the city market to sell cloth and the three children stayed at home. The mother told the children not to open the door to strangers, but not long after she left, the Wolf came. The Wolf disguised itself as a grandmother and used various tricks to fool the three children to open the door.

In the beginning, the Wolf Grandmother was also 'responsible' and took good care of her three children. But in the middle of the night, the oldest sister seemed to hear Grandma eating so, she asked Grandma, 'What are you eating?'

'I'm eating peanuts,' said Grandma.

'Can I have some?' said the sister.

Grandma was silent, as if she was thinking, and the noise of eating stopped. After a while, there was another 'crunch, crunch'. The sister asked, 'Grandma, what are you eating?'

'Fried beans,' Grandma replied.

'I want to eat some too,' said the sister.

'Grandma' handed some to the sister, but when she took them in her hand, they felt sticky and prickly, like finger bones. The sister touched the bed again and she found that her little sister and brother had disappeared. Then she understood that the grandmother had eaten her brother and sister and was about to eat her too.

As a background to the story, we can see that the father was absent in the army and the mother was no doubt stressed from looking after three children on her own. The mother might be an idealised figure for the child, a figure who cannot be attacked or turned bad in the child's mind. So in fantasy, the grandmother could turn into a horrifying figure, as bad as a wolf. The grandmother had eaten the siblings. There is a sinister feel to this 'crunch, crunch', which has echoes with the giant in 'Jack and the Beanstalk', where the giant talks of 'grinding bones to make his bread'.

In the usual Little Red Riding Hood story, the big bad wolf eats the grandmother and Little Red Riding Hood too, but in the end they are rescued. It's a woodcutter in the French version, but a hunter in the Brothers Grimm and traditional German versions, who comes to the rescue with an axe and cuts open the sleeping wolf's stomach. Little Red Riding Hood and her grandmother emerge shaken, but unharmed. Then they fill the wolf's body with heavy stones. The wolf awakens and attempts to run away, but the stones cause him to fall down and die. The woodcutter or the hunter could represent the strong father figure for the child who protects the child from harm. But in the Chinese version, the father was absent and the ending was not a happy one, as my correspondent indicated.

The grandparents are involved much more in looking after grandchildren in China compared with Western grandparents. Especially after the one-child policy instituted in China in the 1980s, couples in this generation have parents and parents-in-law who all want to be involved in looking after this one precious child.

In the version of the story recorded by Charles Perrault in the seventeenth century, a young girl is instructed by her mother to carry supplies through a dark forest to her ill grandmother. On the way, she encounters a wolf who ultimately fools her into believing he is her grandmother and then eats her. (She was pretty naive, wouldn't we think now, telling the wolf where her grandmother lived.) In the Brothers Grimm version, Little Red Cap, as she is called, has a doting grandma who would refuse her nothing. The little girl wears the red velvet cape Grandma gave her to the exclusion of any other coat and she willingly takes cake and wine to her sick grandmother, being warned by her mother not to leave the path (of good behaviour) and not to be nosy in Grandma's house. Along the way, Red Riding Hood meets the wolf and in her fearless and naive way gives him detailed instructions about getting to Grandma's house. Well, what good luck, thinks the wolf. He easily persuades the little girl that her Grandma would love a little bunch of fresh woodland flowers, then he hurries off to the Grandma's house. The rest, as they say, is history, although when Red Riding Hood eventually has a huge bunch of flowers, she finds Grandma's door open and she has a gut feeling that all might not be well. For the wolf, first course has been Grandma and then he gobbles up the little girl and falls asleep, snoring loudly. Enter the brave huntsman, delighted to find his old enemy the wolf so incapacitated. He snips open the wolf's stomach and out pop the little girl and her grandmother, somewhat frightened but apparently unscathed by their ordeal. They all dance with delight, the hunter takes home the wolf's skin, Granny has her cake and wine, and the little girl vows never to stray from the path again. A moral tale indeed.

The story is often read as a simple warning against straying from the 'normal' path, a message to children about listening to their parents, or even a confirmation that evil does lurk, wolf-like, in the trees. These traditional readings of the surface material, however, seem too simple, too readily accepted. They don't delve deep enough. Shall we do a bit of digging? Can we consider the idea that the wolf may be the other side of Grandmother, lurking in the forests? Well, let's take this narrative for a walk. What do these stories in their differing versions have in common?

The fairy/folk tale universe is inhabited by character archetypes, such as those seen here in the form of Little Red Riding Hood and the wolf, who embody unconscious, 'eternal' psychic forces and processes. If we take a little leap and start to imagine that fairy tales can be considered as raw archetypal material, hardly influenced by the conscious mind at all, then where can we go next?

Little Red Riding Hood, then, is the classic female figure, the 'Angel in the House,' unquestioning, willing, and virginal. (A tad curious, as her mother instructs her not to peep into the dark corners.) Innocent and touching in her naivety, even a little stupid, she doesn't hesitate to volunteer information to the very first wolf she encounters. Do we consider there may be an unconscious motivation here?

The wolf, on the other hand, in one reading is the classic base male—representative of the id, he is predatory, driven by instinct, and hungry with desire. But perhaps Little Red Riding Hood and the wolf mirror one another—both masculine and feminine counterparts to the same character? Or perhaps good old Granny is the other side of the coin in the fairy tale? Dark waters indeed. So in fantasy, the grandmother could turn to a horrifying figure, as bad as a wolf, an 'old hag', as she did in the Finnish tale. As Freud said in his thoughts about 'the uncanny', 'it is nothing new or foreign, but something familiar and old, established in the mind that has been estranged only by the process of repression'.

Because the wolf might be a manifestation of her repressed and dormant feelings about the 'goodness' of her grandmother, Little Red Riding Hood recognises the animal when she reaches Grandma's house, allowing herself to question his 'big ears' and 'big legs,' but she is reluctant to piece together the whole. Turning a very blind eye, you might say. The hungry wolf gobbles up the young girl, feasting on her innocence. He gobbled up Granny too. So we might think that the idea of a 'good granny' morphs into a granny who can gobble up her grand-daughter. She has in any event been a rather passive-aggressive figure, living in a dense forest, needing food—and Red Riding Hood's mother was somewhat remiss in sending her daughter unprotected into this situation. Safeguarding issues would abound today.

Among the fifty-eight versions of this story there is even a modern one, an animated cartoon called *Red Hot Riding Hood*, which was released during the Second World War. In 1994, it was voted number seven of the fifty greatest cartoons of all time by those in the animation field. She remains perennially popular, as we can see, in many incarnations.

The story begins with the standard version of Little Red Riding Hood. The characters all feel tired of this stale and derivative staging of the story and demand a fresh approach (as do we all, perhaps). The annoyed narrator accedes to their demands and starts the story over again, in a contemporary urban setting. The narrator explains that Little Red Riding Hood (now portrayed as an adult) is an attractive performer in a nightclub in Hollywood, under the stage name Red Hot, and the wolf, now a Hollywood swinger, follows Red to the club where she is performing. He brings her to his table and tries wooing her, but she wants nothing to do with him. Red escapes the wolf, saying she is going to her grandma's house, but the wily wolf manages to get there first. Grandma's place is a penthouse at the top of a skyscraper and Grandma is a highly oversexed woman, who falls for the wolf. He tries to escape, but Grandma blocks the exit. She locks the door, drops the key down the front of her dress and poses provocatively for him. She puts on some bright red lipstick and a chase scene ensues. But whenever the wolf tries to get out, Grandma waits behind the door with lips puckered up for a kiss. He finally makes his escape by jumping out of a window, severely injuring himself and swearing he is done with women. This grandma is no passive woman but could be seen as provocative and a 'bad' granny.

In huge contrast, Bruno Bettelheim in his book *The Uses of Enchantment* (1976), talks of a charming, 'innocent' young girl swallowed by a wolf in an image which impresses itself indelibly on the mind. In *Hansel and Gretel*, the witch only planned to devour the children; in *Little Red Riding Hood*, both grandmother and child are actually swallowed up by the wolf. So maybe it's not too much of a stretch to suggest that the usual granny figure is swallowed whole, turning into a wolf, and perhaps that is why there is a perennial fascination with this story. Andrew Lang, one of the most erudite and astute students of fairy tales, remarks that if all variants of *Little Red Riding Hood* ended the way Perrault concluded his, we might as well dismiss it simply as a moral tale. This would probably have been its fate if the Brothers Grimm had not boosted its popularity.

The threat of being devoured is the central theme of *Little Red Riding Hood*, as it is of *Hansel and Gretel*. The same basic psychological constellations which recur in every person's development can lead to the most diverse human fates and personalities, depending on what the individual's other experiences are and how they interpret them. Similarly, a limited number of basic themes depict in fairy stories quite different aspects of the human experience. All depend on how such a motif is elaborated and in what context events happen. *Hansel and Gretel* deals with the difficulties and anxieties of the child who is forced to give up their dependent feelings for the mother and free themselves of the wish to eat her up. In her own home, Little Red Riding Hood, protected by her parents, is the untroubled child who is quite able to cope. At the home of her grandmother, who is herself infirm, the same girl is helplessly incapacitated by consequence of her encounter with the wolf, even cooperating with him in finding Granny. This granny is one that she *wants* to get swallowed up, it seems.

Hansel and Gretel think nothing of eating the house that symbolically stands for the bad mother who has deserted them (who forced them to leave home) and they do not hesitate to burn the witch to death in an oven as if she were food to be cooked for eating (as she would have cooked them). As far as the literal meaning of *Little Red Riding Hood* goes, the wolf doesn't do anything that doesn't come naturally—it devours 'food' simply to feed itself. And it is common for a man to kill a wolf, although the method used in this story is unusual.

Little Red Riding Hood's home is one of abundance, which, since she is way beyond the kind of greed showed by Hansel and Gretel, she gladly shares with her grandmother by bringing her food. The world beyond the parental home is not a threatening wilderness through which she can't find a path. Outside her home there is a well-known road, from which, her mother warns, one must not stray.

While Hansel and Gretel have to be pushed out into the world, with just a crust of bread, Little Red Riding Hood leaves her home willingly. She is not afraid of the outside world but recognises its beauty, and therein lies a danger in such an unquestioning narrative. If the world beyond home and duty becomes too attractive, it may induce a return to proceeding according to the pleasure principle, which, we assume, Little Red Riding Hood had relinquished due to her parents' teachings in favour of the reality principle—and then destructive encounters may occur. The grandmother may turn bad, into the wolf.

This quandary of standing between duty and pleasure is explicitly stated when the wolf says, 'See how pretty the flowers are which are all around you. Why don't you have a look around? You don't even hear how beautifully the little birds are singing. You walk along with single-mindedness and concentration as if you were going to school, while everything out here in the woods is merry, happy and bright.' This is the same conflict between doing what one likes to do and what one ought to do, which Red Riding Hood's mother had warned her about at the outset when she admonished her daughter to walk straight to her destination. She is aware of her daughter's proclivity for straying off the beaten path and for spying into corners to discover adult secrets, those of mothers and grandmothers alike, as all children are prone to do.

The wolf represents all the antisocial, animalistic tendencies within ourselves, I suggest, and within our 'beloved' grannies. By giving up the school-age child's virtues of 'walking single-mindedly' as she should, Little Red Riding Hood reverts to the pleasure-seeking child. By falling in with the wolf's suggestions, she has also given the wolf the opportunity to devour her grandmother. Even a four-year-old can't help wondering what Little Red Riding Hood is up to when she gives the wolf specific directions on how to get to her grandmother's house. What is the purpose of such detailed information, the child wonders to herself, if not to make sure that the wolf will find the way? Only adults who are convinced that fairy tales don't make sense can fail to see that the little girl's unconscious is working overtime to give the other side of Good Grandmother away.

Grandmother, too, is not free of blame. A young girl needs a strong mother figure for her own protection and as a model to imitate. But Red Riding Hood's grandmother is carried away by her own needs beyond what is good for the child, and we are told that there was nothing she would not have given the child. It would not have been the first or last time that a child so spoiled by a grandmother runs into trouble in real life. Whether it is mother or grandmother—that is, mother once removed—it is fatal for the young girl if this older woman abdicates her own attractiveness to males and transfers it to the daughter by giving her a too attractive red cloak. The emphasis is on the colour red, symbolising violent emotions.

This struggle between her conscious desire to do the right thing and the unconscious wish to win out over her (grand)mother is what endears the girl and the story to us and makes her so supremely human. Like many of us when we were children and caught in inner ambivalences that, despite our best efforts, we could not master, she tries to push the problem onto somebody else: an older person, a parent or parent substitute. But by thus trying to evade a threatening situation, she nearly gets destroyed by it. Grandmother then turns back into a rescuer, in the Brothers Grimm version.

Many adults today tend to take literally the things said in fairy tales, whereas they should be viewed as symbolic renderings of crucial life experiences. The child understands this intuitively, though they do not 'know' it explicitly. An adult's reassurance to a child that Little Red Riding Hood did not 'really' die when the wolf swallowed her is experienced by the child as a condescending talking down. (See Chapter 2 where children appreciate granny not talking down to them and using 'baby language'.)

Can a Russian version throw some light on what we're thinking about here? Consider the Russian tale of Baba Yaga, the Mother of Witches, who appears in many Russian folk tales. The most famous is *Vasilisa the Fair*. Young Vasilisa is sent to the house of Baba Yaga by her wicked stepmother, who secretly wishes that the witch would eat the girl. The witch's house is guarded by the three riders of death and her servants are three pairs of cut-off hands. Baba Yaga asks the girl to do a lot of fairly meaningless tasks, but Vasilisa does them without questioning. In the end, Baba Yaga rewards her, while her stepmother and stepsisters get burned to ashes. Vasilisa marries a prince—shades of Cinderella here?

So Baba Yaga is neither good nor bad. She has no children but Vasilisa always addresses her as 'the grandmother'. *Baba* means both grandmother and old woman and *Yaga* means a witch. She looks like an ugly old woman, her house is a wooden hut and it stands on a pair of giant chicken legs. It has no windows and the gates are made of human bones. Baba Yaga is the goddess of the hearth, the domestic kitchen witch who knows the secret ingredients made from plants and herbs. Here we have the old hag grandma. Many of these grandmas were drowned as witches. In 1736, the UK Parliament rescinded the witch trials law, thus making 'ducking' of suspected witches illegal. But old customs, it seemed, died hard and it took some time for this to fade away.

My favourite version of the Little Red Riding Hood stories is the one in the children's book *The Jolly Postman* where the Big Bad Wolf is served a notice by a firm of solicitors for impersonation (of Granny) and false imprisonment, although another fun one comes in Roald Dahl's *Revolting Rhymes*, where Red Riding Hood quickly takes out a pistol from her knickers, kills the wolf and makes him into a coat. Stories of what became of the true grandmother vary. Some state that she was 'swallowed whole' and thus freed from the wolf's insides with ease, others state that she died inside his stomach. It would indeed be a death-dealing place to end up—and that is what happens when Granny who is 'good' gets swallowed up and becomes 'bad' (see Chapter 6). In truth, despite her fame, nobody is ever very interested in the grandmother herself (except us, for the purposes of thinking about grannies)—it's all about the wolf with his big eyes, big ears, and, of course, his very big teeth. But, importantly, the wolf might indeed be the other side of the sweet grandma coin, as we suggest here.

Does this give us a clue to what might be happening outside in the world of grandmothers? In all these stories, the wicked wolf leaps on Little Red Riding Hood and gobbles her up.

So let's try not to gobble up the stereotype of grandma but arrive at something more nuanced. We need to listen and look and come to some more balanced conclusions, rather like the characters who asked the narrator for a more up-to-date story, which came out as 'Red Hot'. Things are usually not quite as simple as they may seem. We are all a patchwork of personalities, as the sixteenth-century philosopher Michel de Montaigne suggested, and it makes for a more interesting look at dear old grandma. We are less a symphony than a cacophony of selves. Rigid views and simplistic solutions are not aspects of a spacious mind, a mind that can look at aspects of a theme from multiple points of view.

CHAPTER 6

The deep, dark wood: enter the 'Bad Granny'

In which we see how she can morph ... like Red Riding Hood's granny

In this chapter, we look at stories of estrangement. We have narratives of grannies who have found the path less primrose and more thorn, less idealised and more denigrated, involving law, access, or children used as weapons, in a competition which of course does not help the children in any way. Songs of innocence about a new state are sadly modified by experience. Sons, lovers and daughters-in-law? The classic oedipal triangle—mother, father, child—where triangulation, the accepted method for looking at research from several points of view, may be used (or abused) in a way where one person seeks to control a three-person interpersonal situation for their own benefit. As we'll see here, it often involves threats of exclusion, especially of grandparents, resulting in 'grandparental alienation'.

But grandparents, as many people agree, are at the heart of children's lives. The UK government set up a Childhood and Families Ministerial Task Force in 2010. Ten years before that, Grandparents Apart UK was set up. The group's aim was to put the children first and conflict second, with a mission to help parents reduce legal costs, the inevitable stress of separation, and thus help reduce the pain for the whole family, parents and children alike. This chapter will clarify how this may play out in the

89

lives of ordinary families. The pain may and very often does live on in the next generation.

It's difficult to express the importance of grandparents in a child's life. They may be the children's number one carers, but for too long they haven't had a role to play as far as the law is concerned. When there are troubles in a household, for example a parent is unable to look after their kids due to a drug problem, grandparents are often first to step in and help out. However, recent research has shown that older grandparents, even if they are physically able, find the strain of being solely responsible for their grandchildren makes them feel older rather than younger, as previous thinking would have it. Today's grandparents tend to be older but still fitter than in previous generations. Is this universally true in Western culture? Mothers have babies later, when grannies are older. Of course, people are living longer so there are more years to spend with one another.

Children can grow up to be anti-social or good citizens and much of that comes down to what happens to them in childhood. When parents split up and children are involved, it's not the role of grandparents to take sides. Their role is to mediate and to act in the best interests of the children, which is tricky but ultimately possible.

Courts and social services need to give grandparents more consideration when making assessments about children's lives. They can't underestimate the loving and supportive role grandparents can play. But many parents seem not to appreciate this. As Hilary Mantel said, the cold wind of childhood may blow and make the current children shiver.

The breakup of the parents

One of greatest pains encountered in family life may be the breakup of parents. That can often be followed by the breakup of children's relationship with their grandparents. As a grandmother, I found myself suddenly thrust into the results of family problems in my oldest son's marriage that I wasn't privy to, only feeling the increasing tensions rising in what had been a close family with regular dinners and outings, weekly childcare, sometimes more often, holiday celebrations, birthdays, open-house days at school, reading and storytelling to a grandchild's grade school class. Together with my husband, a writer and theatre person, I loved taking care of our two grandsons, aged four and six, and we did so weekly, sometimes more often, depending on the family needs. Both my husband and I worked full time in the arts, in the theatre and as writers, affording us flexibility and creativity and not much else! We thrived on creativity and adored our grandsons and worked closely with them—painting, singing, playing musical instruments, making puppets, and putting on plays of their own making in the living room after dinner. It was as natural as breathing.

Because of the frequency of our contact, we became aware of growing tensions between my son and his wife. As my son grew more tense and short-tempered, the boys began to cry when he came to pick them up after we'd been babysitting them. One of the last memories I have was of my oldest grandson becoming hysterical and being dragged to the car, and roughly strapped into his child's seat as he was screaming. Care taking also meant grieving, both for the children and for us. My husband and I tried to speak with our son but he and his wife were unwilling to speak with us about our concerns. The children's upset was none of our business, they said. Finally, we were informed we would have no relationship with them whatsoever. We lived in the same area, within a fifteen- to twenty-minute drive of each other.

We didn't understand, but we knew enough to respect their request, and in seeking counselling for ourselves became convinced that if we expressed our concern and upset we would only be pushing them further away. I knew nothing about grand-parents' rights, and even when I discovered them, I was afraid to pursue them given how threatening I found my son's behaviour. He's a very different man than his father, I think, I hope. His father, with whom we lived only briefly, was a very violent man, so much so that I was hospitalised from his attempt to suffocate me with a pillow late one night in bed while I was four months pregnant with our daughter. The next day he beat me up, kicking my feet out from under me, and then kicking me in the stomach before he ran out of the door crying. That landed me in the hospital. My good Catholic upbringing, which told me marriage was for life and I should stick with it, almost got us killed. Mark's father tried to kill himself and our son when Mark was three months old. I brought up Mark and his sister as a single parent.

The end result of my son and daughter-in-law's difficulties was the sudden cut-off of all relationships. The pain comes when children are used as pawns and payback for ancient events that preceded their birth, or that happened when they were young children and had little to no choice in which household they lived, no matter their objection. Divorce courts and mediation are commonly accepted means for addressing this painful situation within families; even their birth they had no part in and as children, they have no control over.

Paying back often means paying forward. When a grandparent loses touch with their grandchildren, it is, as this account shows, absolutely heartbreaking. Children and grandparents are left feeling confused and vulnerable. It's like a bereavement, but without any closure. As another contributor said:

I know myself how easily it can happen. My daughter died of breast cancer, leaving two young children behind. After a few years, their dad met a new woman and moved down south with the kids. His new partner didn't want anything to do with us and we were gradually cut out of our grandkids' lives to the point where we had to hire a lawyer. Thankfully, everything was sorted out in the end despite the expense, but we'll never forget the pain and hurt.

A better end to that heartbreaking story. But that is not the case for everyone.

I know of so many similar devastating tales. There was one woman who lost her daughter to a brain tumour. In the aftermath of her death, emotions were running high and she fell out with the paternal family, resulting in her losing contact with her grandkids. She contacted the charity Grandparents Apart UK (see above) and they helped arrange a mediation session, which resulted in a reconciliation.

Another woman who fell out with her daughter was banned from seeing her five grandchildren and later found out they were being ill-treated in an abuse case. Many others spend the final years of their lives in despair at being unable to see their flesh and blood grow up and share in their experiences. As Michel de Montaigne felt, strong pains grow from the idea of a fixed personality. Or as Ptolemy, the Greek astronomer, was convinced, all the planets, including the sun, revolved around the earth. Can fixed personalities, like fixed ideas, begin to change?

Alienation and estrangement

Using grandchildren as pawns and weapons of control against grandparents, as my contributor above indicated, is a complex form of adult bullying which has reached epidemic proportions in our narcissistic culture. Grandparent alienation is considered to be a severe form of combined child and elder abuse. It is not a solution for breaking past cycles of bullying and domestic abuse, it is simply the substitution of one form of abuse for another, a particularly insidious form of domestic abuse.

Sons, lovers, and daughters-in-law. Does Freud's good old Oedipus complex have relevance now in the twenty-first century? Does every boy want to kill his father and marry his mother? As quantum physicist Carlo Rovelli said, Oedipus is the only detective story where the detective turns out to be the murderer. Is this any help to us now when we think about grannies? While the meme presented by twentieth-century paediatrician and psychoanalyst Donald Winnicott about being 'good enough' has passed into somewhat common usage, how can we think about the opposite meme, of being 'bad enough' via a transition into a realm from which there is often no turning back? While 'good enough' entails times when not good enough can veer back into repair and carrying on, bad enough has a more irrevocable ring. It is difficult to defend the self against a blow for which one is not prepared, and it can induce profound feelings of shame in a grandmother (and of course in a grandfather too, but that is not my focus here). They may fall out of the lives they hoped they would have as grandparents, into a new and profoundly painful daily existence. Is there any way of recovering a lost sense of vibrancy, of fun? No reliable answers exist but an unendurable truth may result. There may be fear and a sense of fragility on both sides, often masked by aggression and even in some cases bullying. War breeds war, lack of forgiveness breeds war, exploited resentments, treasured grievances. If we don't learn to forget a wrong as soon as it's done or said, if we don't all, privately and collectively, draw a line below the past every day of our lives, we're going to be sunk.

The text here shifts and slides depending on what you are bringing to the text, to the table where negotiations may or may not begin to take place. Jane Jackson set up the Bristol Grandparents Support Group (BGSG) in 2007 when she and her husband lost contact with their grand-daughter after their son's divorce, but as the counsel for grief goes, don't run away from your grief but towards it, like the buffalo running towards the storm, unlike the cow that runs away and can never run fast enough. Don't live there either, in the grief zone, which is a dangerous place. This feeling of loss is only one story, one feeling, and even something as simple as doing a small task may have a neurological effect, impacting the brain and changing the neurological circuits to a more benign cycle. Nevertheless, as easy as this may be to say, the words may have little consolation for bereaved grandparents, at least for a time.

Jane said, 'As so often when these things happen to us, we look for help and support. It was something I had never heard of before it happened to us and I couldn't find any, all voices were silent, so I decided to set up my own support. To date I have been contacted by over eight thousand grand-parents. Many grandparents say they don't know why this has happened and they feel ashamed that it has. Many won't talk to anyone about it. To my knowledge, seven grandparents have taken their own lives as a result. It is not only grandmothers who suffer this living bereavement: gender is irrelevant, both grandads and grandmothers suffer equally.'

Shame: such a debilitating and overwhelming condition. The previous formation of the self undergoes a radical re-presentation, there has been a 'confiscation' of an ideal as well as an idea of the self in objective awareness. It's crucial to take on board that, in the myth, Narcissus was entranced by his image, not by his self. When 'grandparent alienation' takes place, the image and status of the would-be grandparent, the granny in this instance, take a huge knock. She loses her sense of self in the reflecting pool and is in danger of drowning. She may feel this chronic sense of shame to be the result of her own failure and she may not want to let others know, but this is quite often the result of the pressured acceptance of another's projected shame. Or is it the result of some combination of self and other? It is vital not to live in a maelstrom of hopelessness and paralysis—this is weather, it can change, it can be helped by bearing witness to one's own and others' pain and grief. After some time it is often that the grief 'lets go' of the grandmother.

Imagine what it is like for grandchildren who have been brought up by their grandparents and suddenly they no longer see them. This is the biggest fear for all grandparents, that their grandchildren will think they don't love them anymore. Or that their grandchildren will forget them. 'I love you, Granny, but Mamma thinks you are bad, Mamma thinks you are not nice.' The phrase 'parental alienation' is now in current use, but 'grandparental alienation', as I said, could also usefully be added to the lexicon.

There are, of course, some grandparents who should not have anything to do with their grandchildren and, as I say later, this can be explored through mediation and supervised access. This is a huge subject in its own right, beyond the remit of this book. In fifteen years of speaking to grandparents, Jane Jackson says she could count on one hand those whom she might question as having issues that might not make them appropriate for the role. As she says, 'I would never put them in a "bad" granny category', but this is how they may be characterised by one or both of the adults whose children are prevented from having contact with them. As she emphasises, 'BGSG's job is to give support and not to be judgemental.' At the time of writing, one of the site's patrons had just launched a petition calling for the rights of grandchildren and it had already garnered more than twenty thousand signatures. It is entitled 'A Grief Observed'.

A report conducted by a firm of London solicitors stated that one in seven grandparents were denied contact with their grandchildren. As there are fourteen million grandparents in the UK alone, you can see that it is a huge issue.

When Jane set up the site, she thought this happened only in separation/divorce situations, but it became very clear, very quickly, that denial of contact is a result of many different scenarios. It can be a problem with drug/alcohol dependency, domestic abuse within the home, bereavement or family fall-out, or simply (though never simple) personality issues, where adult children decide to cut family members out of their lives. There are cases where the adult families have moved, with their families, to another part of the country, leaving no forwarding address. Or they may live close by but out of all contact. Such a silence is very nearly insupportable for the grandparents, and for grannies in particular. This in no way denies the pain that a grandfather can feel too, but that is another as yet untold story.

In the struggle for 'grandchildren's rights', voices, united, may break the silence. It is estimated that at least two million children in the UK are denied contact with their grandparents due to family breakdown. This is not specific to the UK, however, it is a global problem, an international tragedy and a disgrace. No one escapes the hurt.

Every child has the right to a loving and caring relationship with their grandparents, unless it is proven unsafe for the child in the ways I have indicated above. This may be explored through mediation and supervised access.

When you are faced with such a heartbreaking situation, you think it is only you, that no one else is experiencing your feelings of desolation, but of course you are not alone. As Jane Jackson says, 'The grandparents that I have spoken to all say the same thing, that to be able to talk to others is so helpful—before they felt so isolated.' The role of the grandparent is just like that of the first-time parent: no one tells you how to do it, you do it by making mistakes and learning from those mistakes. The trouble is, when you make mistakes it can have catastrophic consequences.

A wrong word or a misunderstood look can sometimes be enough for it to start to fall apart. In a perfect world, we would all be respectful of one another, make allowances, be caring, be kind, as Philip Larkin said, 'while there is still time'. But sadly this is not a perfect world, people are busy, they are anxious, the outlook is uncertain, but we *all* still need other human beings in our lives.

A difficult early history may be revisited and acted out in the current family, at an unconscious level. Why? Very often it happens around the birth of a baby, either the first or maybe the second, perhaps when postnatal depression descends. Postnatal depression soared in 2020— research from University College London that year found that new mothers were more than twice as likely to experience it during the first lockdown than before the pandemic. One of the major symptoms of postnatal depression may take the form of attacking previously 'good' parent figures who are then informed they 'did' things they don't remember doing. And in any case, even if they 'did' and they can't recall it, is it not more 'normal' to forgive and forget and move on rather than hold a grudge which continues for years? Is that 'good' for the children?

Traumatic reactions to early childhood events may repeat: the shock is passed on and the story is retold, but from another point of view, as with Holocaust transmission. Science has shown us that the trauma suffered by Holocaust survivors is capable of being passed on to their children and their children's children. This of course is the clearest sign that one person's life experience can affect subsequent generations. So trauma is transmitted to the child via what is called 'epigenetic inheritance'. Environmental influences including stress and trauma can affect the genes of children and grandchildren.

One of my interviewees was in a concentration camp as a young girl. She told me:

> The potential to behave like the Nazis is within us all. Those of us who have been lucky enough to have had a good enough early experience which enabled us to bind our loving and hating feelings, and have not been subjected to humiliation and denigration, have not needed to act out our hatred and seek revenge for real and/or imagined slights.

Some of us were not and are not so lucky. Disbelief, fear and the heartfelt wish for it all to be a bad dream are common and classic features of trauma. The events are indigestible. John Bowlby's attachment theory taught us about the importance of secure parental foundations and presence in forming stable ongoing identities (see judithedwards.co.uk, attachment e-lectures). Insecure, anxious, and avoidant attachments can lead either to isolation or to hanging on to relationships that mimic those insecurities experienced in early life. Despair can exert a gravitational pull and those who succumb to it may live in the dark. But as somebody once said, there is not a dark switch, only a light switch. Can we switch on the light in the dark?

In these bitter family civil wars, where dreams turn into nightmares, one side has all the power and it's not usually the grandmother, in spite of D. H. Lawrence's *Sons and Lovers*, a salutary story about a mother's power and her son's undoing. Paul falls in love with Miriam Leivers, who lives on a farm not too far from the Morel family. They carry on an intimate but purely platonic relationship for many years. Mrs Morel does not approve of Miriam and this may be the main reason that Paul does not marry her. He constantly wavers in his feelings towards her.

Paul meets Clara Dawes, a suffragette who is separated from her husband, through Miriam. As he becomes closer with Clara and they begin to discuss his relationship with Miriam, she tells him that he should consider consummating their love and he returns to Miriam to see how she feels. Paul and Miriam sleep together and are briefly happy, but shortly afterwards Paul decides that he does not want to marry Miriam and so he breaks off the relationship. Miriam still feels that his soul belongs to her but realises that he loves his mother the most.

Paul begins to spend more time with Clara and they begin a passionate affair. However, she does not want to divorce her husband and so they can never be married. Paul's mother falls ill and he devotes much of his time to caring for her. When she finally dies, he is broken-hearted and, after a final plea from Miriam, goes off alone at the end of the novel. Devoted love for mother was not a solution but the undoing of any happiness he might have experienced long term.

Estranged grandparents have no weapons—if the decision is made to exclude them, that's it, despite mediation. Jenny, for example, told me how much her son's family had depended on her when their son was born and how delighted and fulfilled that had made her feel. That memory caused her acute pain because it all unaccountably (at least to her) ceased a few months after the first grandson's birth. She woke up to smell not the coffee but the cordite. What happened? What had exploded in her face? And what happened perhaps in her daughter-in-law's earlier life to cause such a drastic and possibly repetitive rupture? The dream ended and a nightmare began. The threat of erasure from the lives of her grandson and his family became actual for Jenny.

Here we can see the action of scapegoating writ large: it begins with accusation and of course can end in murder, or suicide as in some of the very sad cases where grannies' hopes have been dashed, often way beyond their rational understanding. Many feel suicidal; few act it out, thankfully. But it can drain away hope and optimism. Our experiences colour everything. The events of the past can have a profound effect on how we see our lives now and what we choose to believe about our world. Our past experiences can also influence our emotional reactions and responses to present events. A brighter future can seem like a pipe dream. Each of us reacts to stimulus based on what we have learned in life. It depends on who has charge of the narrative. While 'narrative coherence' can seem to be an advantage, any narrative can be controlled in order to exclude events which do not fit a current view. Melanie Klein found that people's 'memories' of their parents became more benign over the years, as they could manage different parts of themselves, the difficult as well as the more acceptable, and their parents. A. N. Wilson in his biography of Queen Victoria shows how the young queen's view of her mother varied over the years, as she was affected by different people in her life who wished to influence her in contrary ways. As a grandmother, she acted out very similar scenarios to the ones she had abhorred in her own mother.

There is no right or wrong to it; it is simply, or complicatedly, the result of past experience. Later, when our strong feelings have passed, we may be surprised at our reactions. Yet when we face a similar situation, again our reactions may be the same. When we understand those experiences, we can come that much closer to understanding those reactions and consciously change them. Yes, it's hard work, but it's worth it in the longer run, as my work with parents and grandparents over the years has shown.

When things between you and your in-law seem impossible … sometimes you just need to laugh. If you can. So enjoy your life and let yourself laugh. Easier said than done, of course, when our default position may be to resort to sad thoughts. Cultivating others in your 'garden of relationships' in these circumstances is tough indeed. 'Hell's Grannies', a Monty Python sketch from 1971, shows the famous actors dressed in flowery hats and black coats, running rampage in the streets, shrieking and frightening the populace, kicking random passersby, overturning phone boxes. They say they're in it for 'the violence, the prestige, the gifts'. It's worth a watch when you're feeling down.

When the conventional rosy picture is of grandparents at the centre of every family party, there can be stigma attached to estrangement, with some people unable to confess the truth even to their friends. They may live in a perfect storm of despair. One such grandmother fell apart emotionally when she saw in a newspaper a 'famous' person holding her newborn grandchild.

Grandmothers may feel such pain, especially when they recognise that they originally may have caused the rift and deeply regret it. Florence, for example, wrote: 'It gives me some relief to be able to share the pain I'm experiencing. Unfortunately, due to some harsh words I regrettably said about a woman my daughter-in-law works for, things went sour between us. Now I have been robbed of watching my little granddaughter grow up.

I have made a mistake, but surely this punishment is too harsh? If anyone can think of advice, I would be glad to receive some as I am desperate.'

Alas, there is no tried and tested way to build a bridge, to kiss and make up when relationships have ruptured beyond repair. How do you apologise when you have no idea what exactly you have done wrong beyond a few 'harsh words'? We are all familiar with the well-known saying 'life is too short'. Well, sometimes in these circumstances, life may seem too long.

Jillian's story

Like Jenny, Jillian had been delighted at the birth of her first grandchild. A disabled woman in her seventies, Jillian visited her daughter-in-law and new grandson in hospital and accompanied them to the hospital when there were concerns about the child's breathing. Jillian felt honoured to be a part of this, and proud. However, because of her disabilities, there were childcaring duties Jillian couldn't manage in a sustained way, even though she did some supervision online with younger members of her profession. Gradually, she felt there was a withdrawal: Granny no longer seemed welcome at any time, and while her son valiantly tried to have a conversation when Granny came round at a prearranged time, her daughter-in-law sat resolutely with her back to them, holding the child so that Granny had just a little glimpse of him. No possibility of sharing here. The lovingly knitted little hat was shrunk in the wash and never worn—love's labours lost, you might say. And pictures show an unsmiling daughter-in-law.

What was going on in her mind? Did she deem the son/mother relationship to be too close? Or was this the result of something from her own childhood, visited on the paternal grandmother? The daughter-in-law had indeed described a harsh and difficult childhood, so perhaps this had been unconsciously revisited and unconsciously reversed so that someone else—the grandmother—felt the traumatic pain originally experienced in the mother's childhood. The daughter-in-law's contact with neighbours who had lost their own grandchild because of a stillbirth only exacerbated an already fraught situation.

When a second child was born, things worsened. Granny did indeed wonder what she had 'done' and whether she could be forgiven if she had inadvertently crossed some line, but there seemed to be no solution, in spite of her requests for 'forgiveness'. Perhaps things had been 'done' on both sides and forgiveness could be a way forward? This couple had met online and married very soon, partly because the son could not be introduced to the daughter-in-law's family until a marriage was on the cards due to her religious background. Such couples who marry so hastily have not had the benefit of friends and family advising them to slow down and they may rush into an instant bond, even having children, and then part. And of course this can then link to grandparent alienation.

Eventually, Jillian's son separated from his wife, whom he thought had become 'mentally unwell' and told Jillian, 'We're the baddies now, Mum.' As I noted earlier, this is a sad outcome of some women afflicted with postnatal depression. 'Right' and 'wrong' were adamantine concepts, so mediation was the next step. 'I was devastated, suicidal at times,' said Jillian. 'Nothing I could possibly have done could have deserved such treatment.' But it was irrevocable. For a time, the children were delivered to their father when their mother was working and he generously allowed Jillian contact with her grandchildren. Jillian formed a strong attachment to them and vice versa. As one of them said when he hid Jillian's coat, 'I want you to stay for ever.' 'I've got a big idea,' said the other. 'We can all live together in Daddy's house.' But that all ended when the daughter-in-law's work ended. Jillian had so many mornings to ponder all this, to learn to tolerate loss, and manage the considerable good also present in her personal world, without letting it fragment into a thousand broken pieces. Admittedly, good is often not simple to find. But she has tried. There is another world there and it is real, if profoundly different from what Jillian had hoped for. Finding is recovering, recovering is recognising, and recognising is accepting, navigating 'the new normal'. It is a long, slow road.

Erick's story

But here is another side of Granny/daughter-in-law conflict. As a boy growing up in Indonesia, Erick Setiawan's dreams were haunted by his grandmother, an all-powerful matriarch who according to him plotted and manipulated to keep her family at loggerheads and made his mother's life a misery. Some children, as he says, are afraid of ghosts or monsters. He was terrified of becoming an orphan and falling into the hands of the devil's concubine. That was one of his mother's names for her mother-in-law, with whom she had a tumultuous relationship for nearly thirty years.

As a child in Indonesia, Erick was far too often mixed up in their conflicts, sometimes used as a pawn by one side while the other side tried to win him over. He secretly believed that his grandmother had magic powers. As a fifth-generation Chinese Indonesian, his grandmother believed in ancestor worship and respect for one's elders, but this became totally turned around once she herself had children. She had to be the centre of attention, and she felt miserable and unwanted unless her sons and daughters were quarrelling, in need of her love and mediation. Dividing and ruling are of course, as we have seen, age-old weapons of conflict.

When the grandmother found out that Erick's father was secretly attending elementary school classes, she made his grandfather throw out his books and cut up his clothes. What a soul-destroying metaphor for his cut-up hopes. And so her tyranny over her family went unchallenged. But then she met Erick's mother, also a Chinese Indonesian but from a very different background. Erick's mother was always a rebel. She wore ultra-cool bleached cut-off jeans, went out with a lot of boys and skipped school to dawdle in record stores listening to her favourite songs.

She met her husband when she was sixteen and she decided to marry him in spite of family disapproval. In photographs taken at the wedding, neither Erick's mother nor his grandmother looks remotely happy. Both perhaps already had a premonition of the battle to come and each was warily measuring up the other. The morning after the wedding, the grandmother fired the opening shot. She took the wedding gifts and claimed them as her own. Bang.

'She deceived me from the start,' Erick's mother confided years later. 'Before the wedding, she pretended to be kind and warm and I fell for it. And then she revealed her true face.' The path of narcissism writ large.

While his rebellious mother struggled to find her footing in the family, the grandmother found countless ways to bully her into submission. She rebuffed her daughter-in-law in front of company by calling her 'spoiled', 'pig-headed', and 'too westernised for her own good'.

Erick's father finally became financially independent. His mother made decisions without consulting her in-laws and spoke to the grandmother only when she felt like it. The grandmother tried to buy Erick's affection with sweets and flatteries. She promised him that he could do whatever he wanted if he lived with her. Most memorably, she told him that his mother loved his younger brother more than she loved Erick (untrue), even though his brother was adopted (also untrue). But the author is honest enough to say that he too would play one off against the other (divide and rule passed on).

His grandmother finally became a figure of total terror in his life and he was filled with dread that if his mother died, his grandmother would be his guardian. But it never happened. Erick moved to the States and her terrifying hold on him dissipated. And his mother? 'She resolved to be the best mother-in-law in the world. My sisters-in-law can happily attest to this.'

This is a sad story indeed. But what would the grandmother have said if she could have told her story?

The emergence of the bad mother-in-law

Here is a story of someone able to laugh at herself.

> When Hope was born, in 1969, my husband took John, our elder child, to his mother for safekeeping, as his Para unit was called to go to Northern Ireland at the start of the Troubles exactly an hour after I had delivered the baby. He had about six hours in which to pack up the house and leave. In those days the hospital stay was seven days for baby number two so when Hope and I came home, a dear friend agreed to come with me to Oxford where my mother-in-law wanted to meet to give me John. We were living near Aldershot. So with my friend, her two little children and baby Hope, we meet at the designated place and mother-in-law arrives with John. To my horror he has been to a barber and given a short back and sides haircut—all his gorgeous baby curls gone without my permission. I cried. I just loved those baby curls. All gone. I've forgiven her, but I've never forgotten it. Bad mother-in-law!

In my research, I found a book which had a balanced view, taking account of both sides of 'the story'. *Reluctantly Related: Secrets to Getting Along with Your Mother-in-Law or Daughter-in-Law* by Deanna Brann is all about the delicate situation of resolving differences between in-laws.

Why is it that in-law relationships can be so challenging? Well, as Dr Brann reminds her readers, in-law relationships are artificial constructs. The central figure in such relationships (the son, in Dr Brann's writing) has become a husband. A new family is established and the roles of mother, son, and daughter-in-law need to take this change into account. But so often, each participant looks at what is happening from their own perspective. Here indeed we have the Oedipus complex writ large, when daughter-in-law 'takes over' from mother.

Dr Brann, a licensed clinical psychotherapist, writes of her own experience with her daughter-in-law, providing an example of a disastrous family Thanksgiving because both she and her daughter-in-law interpreted events from their own perspectives. Both sides of the story are related here and this provides a lead-in to the challenges of the mother-in-law (MiL)–daughter-in-law (DiL) relationship, including the artificiality of the relationship, the different stages of life (generally different generations), the personal history, and the emotional baggage (we each have both and heavy indeed they can be). It is of necessity a joint composition.

Dr Brann introduces four personality types of MiL—Comfortable Carla, Mothering Margaret, Off-the-Wall Wanda, and Uncertain Sara—and four personality types of DiL—Confident Connie, Doubting Donna, Weird Wendy, and Transitioned Tracy. There are also three personality types for the husband/son—Self-Assured Andy, In-the-Middle Michael, and Struggling Steven. I am somewhat wary of stereotypes, but in this case it works as a way of focusing on the particular needs of each character and how a MiL or a DiL can understand where the DiL or the MiL is coming from. It's this under-standing that is critical to making in-law relationships work effectively. Managing expectations, great and small, is important, as is respecting boundaries. The effective use of humour can help as well. It sure helps get out of 'a bad neighbourhood'.

The book contains questionnaires (so that you can identify personality types), patterns of behaviour, and how to deal with them. All very useful stuff.

The unanimous act of violence or exclusion against the scapegoat (in this case grandmother, usually mother of son who is now husband) can almost miraculously restore peace and social cohesion, in a family no less than in a state. Often the 'enemy' outside the gates can be used to project conflict outside rather than in the parental relationship. This was something I was to encounter many times in family work. If we look further, we find that ritualised re-enactments of the scapegoat mechanism can be found in archaic religions in human culture— sacrificial rites and the immolation of the victim come before all else, it seems. While this may seem quite a stretch from 'way back then' to 'grandmothers now', it's also interesting to note that the Hebrew word for 'Satan' (also 'Satan') means adversary or accuser: perhaps we may suggest that there might be a distinctly satanic element at work in the zeal for accusation and prosecution. But similarity as well as difference may be an issue here: often we fight to prove our difference from an enemy who in fact is like us in ways we are eager to deny (what, in the psychoanalytical jargon which we're trying to avoid here, would be called 'projective identification').

These issues will be taken up again in the last chapter, which concludes the book with ideas and ways to go forward about the rethinking of the grandmother meme. Our experiences colour everything. The events of the past can have a profound effect on how we see our lives now and what we choose to believe about our world. Our past experiences can also influence our emotional reactions and responses to present events. Each of us reacts to stimuli based on what we have learned in life. I must emphasise here: there is no right or wrong to it, it is simply the result of past experience.

Between stimulus and reaction exists a fleeting moment of thought. Often (very often) that thought is based on something that has happened to you in the past. Emotional factors may indeed lead to repression, which like the beach ball forced down into the water will bounce up higher when it is released, but this also has the benign effect of making what is remembered manageable.

To quote Jenny again: 'Never a day goes by that I don't think of my son and our grandson. I cannot remember the last time I was truly happy. My very bones ache with the grief of not seeing them both.'

The long game

Let Jane Jackson have the last hopeful word here: it may be 'a long game' but it may come to an end.

> I am now reunited with my granddaughter after fifteen years apart. She is now twenty-two, so the little girl who had been seven arrived at our door as a beautiful young woman, and she fell into my arms as though she had never been away. I was able to tell her that we never stopped loving her, and my heart broke when she replied, 'And I never stopped loving you.'

These children who are unjustifiably estranged never forget their grandparents, they just know that to talk about it will get them into trouble, so they don't. They simply hold the grandparents in their hearts, as their grandparents do them.

CHAPTER 7

Flo and co

In which grandmothers are recalled, over the years

Before starting this chapter, it is salutary and vital to remember those whose grandmothers have been taken from them. One of my correspondents said, 'I have no grandparents, they were all killed in the Holocaust.' So if we have memories, good or bad or somewhere in between, we must give thanks for our good fortune to have been able to have these experiences. We all have stories and most of us are keen to tell them.

Flo: she is the reason, as I said in the Introduction, that I started writing this book and her picture as a young woman is the frontispiece. She deserves her place here, as an icon in my own small world; she stands in my memory alongside my grandad, who was the other half of this narrative. The following is adapted from my previous book, *Pieces of Molly.*

> My grandparents, my mother's parents, lived in a rambling thirties' one-level house, with an outside loo where I sat with dangling legs smelling the odd combination of Elsan fluid, lavender from the bunches hung by my gran above the door, and all our dumped remains. I used to swing my legs, inhale and sing. My father's parents had died long before my birth, father of peritonitis from a rotten unrecognised appendix, misdiagnosed

as constipation by an ignorant family doctor, as my aunt Old Acid (my father's nickname for her) always scornfully said, and mother, perhaps, from the exhaustion of continual childbearing. She had made an unpromising marriage for love and had been virtually ignored for the rest of her life by her rather grand local family, one member of whom had invented shorthand. There was a tantalising tale that somewhere there remained an unread will, which left my father's mother the fortune to which she should have been entitled.

In the one remaining picture of this woman who followed the impulse of her heart and not her material welfare, she looks a little sad. She could never cook, but since they had several maids, a necessary succession of girls indiscriminately called Annie, the family didn't starve. While Dad had nothing complimentary to say about his mother's cooking, whenever he had a sore throat he fell back on her tested and ancient remedy for colds. You could tell he was ill as soon as you opened the back door. A wafting sickly smell of vinegar would hit you in your throat and my mother, who relied on more modern methods, would look on in frank distaste as he soaked a piece of old toast in a warm stew of vinegar, then wrapped the soggy stuff round his neck in a piece of old sheet. Mother knows best.

In the last years before her husband died, my paternal grandmother had apparently long retired from sex and had been carried up and downstairs by my devoted father, her second youngest son, night and morning, to and from her throne in the living room, where he plaited and replaited her hair, winding its heavy coils above her ears. He transferred his allegiance from one queen to another, and it was no doubt a good thing that his mother had died several years before he met his wife. Being in thrall to both would have been tricky, if not impossible.

My grandmother, Flo, was warm and soft. My brother would sit on her knee when he was a little boy, kneading her breasts which were squashy and welcoming, calling them 'her buns'. She laughed with tolerance, and love. Her bedroom smelt of lily of the valley talcum powder, which she let me use too, sprinkled on a large and soft pink powder puff, which lay ceremonially with her silver brush and comb and mirror on the top of the large mahogany dressing table. While baths at home were mostly strictly about cleaning until I was considered old enough to do it for myself, baths in Grannie's soft pink and cream bathroom were languid and warm, as I sat and made huge air bubbles on the surface of the water with her flannel, and exploded them under water in a thousand little beads, so that the flannel seemed as lively as a fish swimming in a heated aquarium.

Gran taught me to knit and I struggled proudly with the thick needles and dropped many stitches, to make pathetic little scarves for my dolls and teddy bears, lopsided and inadequate, which she examined with a critical but kindly eye. My continually imagined projects of perfection as mother of my little family never failed to disappoint me with their sad reality, but she encouraged me to persevere.

She called me 'duckie' and 'pet' and made marvellous caraway seed cake, which we sometimes ate on the lawn, where she warned me not to sit on damp patches under the acacia trees, for fear of getting 'tick dolleroo'. It was only much later when I learned French that I recognised this as a version of the French *tics doloureux*. So I used to sit on her doorstep, tracing my finger over the smooth sunny sill with one hand, a piece of still-warm seed cake in the other, talking and carelessly munching with my mouth open if I wanted to.

There were two crab-apple trees in the primrose wood, and in Gran's cookery book, in a small, yellowed envelope carefully marked 'Crab Jelly', is a handwritten recipe, not her own careful script but neat enough, from a neighbour maybe, who advises washing the crab apples but leaving the stalks so that they just 'peep out' of the water. She uses a strong pillowcase, she says, to drain the pulp all night over a bowl. Squeezing, she warns, must not be done on any account, or you will have a murky result. Next day you boil the juice with a pound of sugar to every pint, and test it as you go to test its jelliness. You must skim it continuously. Those saucers of gelling jam, they strike my inward eye immediately when I read these words set out so long ago. I used to stand by my stirring gran and badger her to test the jam, raspberry, strawberry, marrow or crab, every few minutes, so I could pronounce on the progress of the jam and even more important, lick up the wrinkling contents straight from the saucers as they stood in little rows by the open window.

I sucked in my grandmother's nectar, encased in her soft body like the sugared centre of her favourite Newberry Fruits, full of colour and sweetness. And how was it, I wonder now, that I found her so empathic, when something had gone so wrong between her and her one and only daughter? Was it simply the mellowness of age which made my grandmother so accessible to me, or had the fit between mother and daughter never been good enough? Perhaps I gave her a saintliness which was a contrast with what I experienced at home, with my mother, who apart from anything else never really recovered from the three days of labour she endured giving birth to me.

Gran used to take me on the train from her small village to the local town and I sat in awe, with my legs dangling on the firm seats of the closed carriages which led straight onto the platform of the village station, well-kept and spruce in those days, with only the odd stubborn bit of red valerian challenging life at the foot of the wall outside the ladies' waiting room. The village was reassuringly solid as we walked to the station side by side without talking very much at all, in the dry and dusty air which blew around my feet as I scuffed it up with my sandals. Names like Station Road, Cliff Walk, Kennel Loke and Main Street, both sewed it into normality, a place on the map, and gave it at the same time a sort of mythical status, like a little settlement at the foothills of Mount Olympus. The station and the station master were both in those days necessities before the wholesale arrival of the car and the death of this honourable railway life. Each carriage on the heavily breathing train had six water colour reproductions fixed above the seats, often of local scenes, the marshes and the windmills and the skies with their endless spaces, and little nets above the seats to keep your hat and brolly in. The windows opened and were fixed by a strong leather strap. The station master's firm timetable of whistles and waves gave me great comfort, a sense of something in the world going to plan.

Each station stop was marked by the calm announcement of its name, several times, not by a recorded voice but by a someone in one of the little station offices. It seemed to me like an honourable job, to mark the pilgrimages ordinary people made, and I wondered whether that might be something I could aspire to, in later life.

On rainy days I crouched by the bottom brass-handled drawer of the huge and shining walnut bureau, poring over the old copies of *Picture Post* and *Illustrated London News*, which packed the drawer to the brim, making it hard to open. There were pictures of conflict around the world, of politicians and film-stars, and of those two fairy-tale princesses Elizabeth and Margaret, who seemed in their cuddly cardigans and buttoned shoes so remote and inscrutable and yet as near to me as the sisters I had never had. When my dissatisfactions, real and imagined, with my real parents grew to unmanageable proportions, I would dream of being royal too. Perhaps I shared my mother's aspirations. These little girls, whose pictures had been re-released when their nanny decided to tell her story, were in reality quite a bit older than me. Indeed, the Princess Elizabeth, fourteen years old at the beginning of the war well before I was born, broadcast her empathy to displaced people everywhere, saying she was glad her home, even though it was a palace, had been bombed too, so that she could look the people in the East End of London in the face.

Granny also had a scrapbook full of picture postcards, saved all down the years from when she was a girl, recording the treasured holiday moments of the, to me, unknown old friends and relations, which must indeed have contributed somehow to the sum of human happiness. My Dad too had saved all the postcards I had ever sent him, but bundled haphazardly and held with an elastic band. When my mother died and I had to clear her house in a hurry, I sighed, put them in a black plastic bag for the dustman and have regretted it so many times, not for what they might have told me but because I was throwing away something he had cherished. And in her own way my mother must have cherished them too.

Relegated to the lumber room in Gran's house, and I never knew why, was the little old blue upholstered armchair which my mum had sat on when she was smaller than I was then. I used to go and sit on it in secret. It had a melancholy feel, and whatever history it hid, I felt I could ask no questions about it.

In the main living room, along with little gold-framed oil paintings of marshes, dykes and windmills, landscapes where melancholy music seemed to seep from the shadows, hung her beautiful collection of pale blue painted Chinese plates, fluttering with butterflies and small birds, etched with twigs of extraordinary delicacy, and amassed throughout her married life. When she was an old lady she offered them to me and in my ignorance I refused, saying I could not think of it while she was still alive and they ornamented her life. So she thought them not worthy of any attention, directed in her will that all her goods go up for auction, and my sister-in-law bought the lot. Because of the family rift which plagues each generation of our family, I can no longer even see them now.

Could I have asked you, Gran, about what was going on? If facts are to be believed, there was indeed a lot going on. Would you have said, 'There there, pet, don't you fret yourself'? Could I have let you know what was eroding me from the inside, invading even the softness of my night's sleep in the billowing folds of your second best feather bed? I dream of straining to hear Gran's voice above rushing water, but can't make out what she is trying to say. There there, pet. I'm still here.

Just outside the back door of my grandparents' house, mounted on the fence, was a tin food safe which kept things cool behind its wire-mesh door, and in summer time too there would be a wasp trap or two hanging from the adjacent tree: a jam jar with a spoonful of some sweet bait at the bottom and a paper lid with a one-way-no-exit hole, the greedy wasps buzzed in eagerly and drowned in the nectar they had so desired, and as they died you could hear their mournful buzzing recitative. They can fly forwards, backwards, upwards and downwards, those canny wasps, masters of their little universes, until they are defeated by the baffling inward shutters of a paper lid.

Over the fence was a well-tended orchard plot, where another Mr Smith, this time an old man with teeth stained almost black from a lifetime of tobacco chewing, pruned his apple trees and leaned his bent body on a rake to admire his tidy work. I would kneel on a chair looking out of Gran's dining room window and watch him, raking and chewing, up and down the lines of little trees. If I gave him a small friendly wave, he would nod briefly and carry on.

'Why doesn't he speak to me, Gran?' 'His wife is dead, duckie, and he's probably very sad.' 'But his garden is lovely.' 'Yes.'

Inside the house just next to the back door was the cupboard under the draining board where my grandfather kept the shoe-cleaning stuff: a battalion of little circular gold-lettered tins and graded wooden-backed brushes, all neatly labelled. Black Polish, Black Off, Brown Polish, Brown Off. The smell of that cupboard intoxicated me, it was as magical to me as my old friend linseed putty, and I would watch as he gravely worked up a shine on a row of his stout shoes, my gran's well-worn, high-heeled lace-ups, and my own current pair of buttoned bar-shoes too if I was lucky.

Next to the cupboard and the kitchen sink was the pantry, a walk-in cornucopia of tins holding buns and cakes, jars of jams and marmalades, and a great big white porcelain pot which I still have, which held the pickled eggs and smelt of brine. There were neat piles of green and white china—the best bone china pansy teacups were in a separate china cabinet along with the silver teapot, which I now don't keep as shiny as she once did—and mugs hanging from hooks along the length of the shelves. It was all painted cream, like the kitchen, and seemed to smell of baking, and I could feel satisfied just standing in there, without needing to eat a thing.

In the post-war cookery book that was evidently my grand-mother's bible, as I suppose from the cuttings and jottings she left behind in it, the author offers this sage advice: 'When choosing your culinary wares, let your text be: *Everything in this Kitchen will have to be cleaned*.' The average kitchen, she maintains, contains too many things. With the demise of domestic servants, her maxim is to buy little and replace each broken article only where necessary. Her list of kitchen equipment for a household of about four people looks extensive, but my gran had all these things, from china jelly moulds to fish slices, mincing machines and fish-kettles, all neatly stored away in her own little palace kitchen where she was both queen and servant maid alike.

What a lot of odds and ends accumulate in your kitchen! One of the advertisements at the end of Granny's cookbook advises throwing them all into a saucepan and stewing them for half an hour with a packet of Edwards' desiccated soup, made in three varieties, brown, white and tomato. This, or so the spin had it, would turn your useless scraps into 'a dish of dishes'. The little circular inset picture of a self-satisfied woman in bib and bonnet somehow set the seal on this sinister advice: I can't imagine my gran ever having to stoop so low.

Granny was a member of the Women's Institute and I too faithfully went along to the local village hall to hear about local history and flower drying, and to sing *Jerusalem* at the top of my off-key voice: 'I shall not cease from mental fight, nor shall my sword sleep in my hand.' I bathed in the warm attention of granny and her neighbours, and when my own attention wandered I could wander too, out to play ball on the grass below the high windows, where I could say hallo to passersby. Jam and Jerusalem, a cliché now. What would she have made of WI members posing for a girlie calendar, or Spit the Cherry Stone competitions? Spitting was for kids and we had revelled in it— but for grown-ups? Gran wore a little oval badge, with the letters W and I entwined in its centre, and a rose on the left and a maple leaf on the right. This W and I seemed a harmonious knot to me, just like the reef knots my father used to teach me about: left over right, then right over left. If you crossed the ends the wrong way, what you got was what he called 'a Granny knot', but to me, a Granny knot was good. She, who had the powerful gift of being remembered well by many people, lives on in me. Night night, pet, sleep tight, don't let the fleas bite.

A friend at my convent school had shown me how to make a 'false knot'. First you make a circle of string, just about the size of a skein of wool. I'd seen my father patiently hold these skeins while my mother swiftly rolled off the wool into loose balls and stowed them in her knitting basket. She could do the same job by stretching the skein between the backs of two upright chairs, but it was something both she and my father seemed to enjoy, the rhythmic gentleness of it, somehow binding them at least in those moments into a functioning whole.

This false knot intrigued me from the start. You wind the string around and around your fingers, so it looks as if you're binding them up beyond escaping. Then you lift the two intertwined strands from off your little finger, give a gentle pull and the string against all logic untwists into your original circle. I practised for weeks till I got it down to a certainty, then did my magic over and over again as a comfort when there were other knots which weren't so easy to master. When we are stressed and overwhelmed, as I was increasingly overwhelmed by the relationship between my father and my grandmother, which would prove so problematic, this kind of ritual can settle us down.

The village fete was held once a year on the pleasant pasture they called The Meadow at the front of the house, my own home and country of the heart, bordered on one side by the village school and on the other by the Methodist chapel and an area of tangled blackberry bushes, all now vanished in the thrust of development. All that remains is the stained-glass lantern from the chapel, saved from the demolition by my grandad and now hanging in my hall. Because this was my grandparents' land, I felt a pride of ownership.

To the left and in front of the house, beyond the primrose wood and edged by tall trees, was another meadow, where the blackberry bushes were more accessible and where we would all hover and gather in baskets and punnets the fruit that Gran made into jam, into pies, and solemnly sealed in vacuum jars which were warmed and ready in the oven on bottling day. My dad and grandad hauled down the more inaccessible clusters with their long sticks. Purple lips gave me away and I used to get fed up with the command to pick more and eat less. I would grizzle and groan my way around the field and the adults tended quite rightly to ignore me. My brother was too little to be required to do anything beyond being there, under their eye. Gran would pack the fruit in the jars, fill them with cold water and screw the caps down tight onto their rubber rings. They would sit in polite rows in a pan of water in the slowly heating oven for an hour, or maybe two. Then she would remove them, one at a time, and give each cap an immediate and final screw. It was a satisfying hoarding of the world's bounty.

In her battered cookery book one of the batch of advertisements at the back, all couched in courteous language now long since abandoned in the world of the hard sell, proclaims 'a revolution in fruit bottling'. For one and ninepence you could get a batch of thirty seals and adaptable parchment covers' to use on any old jar you happened to have around. But Granny, proud in her kitchen, used only the best, her fruit didn't need to 'keep indefinitely', pies and crumbles would be scoffed soon enough.

But there's something in me still which responds to the need in those days to preserve and conserve. In the same cookbook are extolled the virtues of a hay box and instructions on how to make one. This fireless cooker came into its own as domestic labour became scarcer after the Great War and when fuel was rationed. You brought your pot of porridge or your beef stew to the boil and then nested it into the hay box where it could go on cooking gently in its own cocooned heat, redundant newspapers and fine hay in a mattress made of old flannel kept your dinner snug, and you could even, it was suggested, decorate the box with paint and cretonne.

At my grandparents' house I slept in a large double feather bed, sinking into its mountain folds as I listened to them listening the Palm Court Orchestra on the radio on Sunday nights in the next room. They had an old record player, just like the one the dog listened to on His Master's Voice, and black shiny records: you wound it up and you could listen to *Scenes from a Persian Market* or Kathleen Ferrier's drowned-soul lament *Blow the Wind Southerly, Southerly, Southerly*, or my favourite *Being a Chum Is Fun, That Is Why I'm One, Always Laughing, Always Gay, Chummy at Work and Chummy at Play* … what a crashing bore this chummy person must have been. I would wind up the handle, put on the disc and stomp around the room in a trance of dance. Then I'd collapse in exhausted delight onto the brown leather settee (they were not called sofas in my grandparents' lower-middle-class milieu).

My questions kept coming up, as they do, well within the normal range of the average enquiring child's mind. Why does a chair have arms, where does the sun go, what makes us die? Are we nearly there, where do our dreams go when we wake up, do you love me? Why does the wind blow? Why? 'Because God made it so' declared exasperated parents and grandparents when I was young, shutting the door on this quest for why, so I kept my struggle inside myself and had to wait for years to know the eternal humanness of these preoccupations. Was someone infinitely larger than me, I wondered, holding a bucket with me as a picture on it?

My grandparents kept chickens and each day my grandmother mixed up in a galvanised pail a warm steaming mash of spuds and bran. I also had a little rocky garden plot—just a raised mound of rather unpromising ashy soil. More interesting to me than growing plants whose pale-green and undernourished stalks sprawled helplessly over the soil and almost never bore flowers was upturning the stones and watching the woodlice, pale grey and unhealthy looking, curl into balls or lumber for cover. If I crouched too long under the shade of the acacia tree on the damp earth my grandmother would come out and admonish me.

Memory, as we must all admit, is a strange and plastic thing. In my memories of my grandmother, she is the woman who stands straight and true, in the middle of the muddle of other thoughts, other feelings. Dear Flo flows on, and would she be surprised at how much she has influenced my whole life?

Here's another (Italian) view on the value of grandparents and how these can change and be appreciated over time.

When I was young we were all anti-everything, but looking back, my sister and I realise how great Nonna was, non-judgemental, and I wish I could tell her now about how I admired her, her taking on a huge amount of responsibility ... We used to go out dancing, having a great time, and she must have worried quite a bit about us, but she never showed it. My lovely Nonna! Every November we put flowers on her grave, and also that of our Great-nonna, who caught me on my knees drinking vodka when I was about eight.

Dancing, dancing, which leads on to the next story ...

Curl up like the new moon

Whenever I think about my Maa Maa,[1] I think about her feet. Reclined on her bed on a hot summer's afternoon ready for

---

[1] Maa Maa is Cantonese for paternal grandmother 嫲嫲 [maa maa]. It is pronounced in a much lower register and should sound distinctly different compared with Ma Ma meaning Mother.

her siesta, her feet—both long *and* wide—would stick out of her two-piece traditional Chinese outfit: a top, buttoned up in butterfly knots to cover her neck, and trousers, loosely fitted in a silky sort of material. Her whole appearance exuded a soft, subdued, demure elegance, her wispy white hair tied up in a bun. Sometimes this effect would be further enhanced by a delicately placed stick hairpin, lending an extra air of old-school elegance. I felt both intimate with and awe-struck by Maa Maa. As a young child, my eyes looked up to heaven and sighed a deep sigh. She felt both very near and very far away. I pined for her.

But something also felt out of place. Her feet, so robust and long, didn't somehow belong to the rest of her body. I had to live with this mystery for a long time before one day, emboldened by the leisure of the summer holiday, feeling relaxed and a little sleepy, with the sight of Maa Maa's feet again poking out at the end of the bed, I finally spoke: 'Maa Maa, your feet are *soooo* big and strong!' I didn't know what to expect for a moment, my wide eyes fixed on her face. My words filled the space all around us, like an elephant in the room. A sharp intake of breath and my heart stopped. Nothing seemed to happen for ages. Then Maa Maa smiled a slow, quiet smile, revealing just a little bit of a gold filling on one side of her mouth, her face wrinkled up even more than usual. It was a sad smile and I was sad I had brought this on. Quietly she began, 'I know, they don't curl up like the new moon.' Still mystified, I tried my hardest to be patient. I didn't want to wait, but in Maa Maa's quiet way, she had set the pace for her own story, and there wasn't much I could do to hurry her on.

The story about Maa Maa's feet in fact only emerged piecemeal. I wonder now if she couldn't tell it all in one go, or if she felt I wasn't yet ready to hear and bear her history; of how she grew up belonging to a last generation of Chinese girls being forced to submit to the cruel custom of foot binding; how she protested and resisted having her feet bound and mutilated. But in exchange for relative freedom and independence, Maa Maa also faced a lifetime of guilt, of betraying her sisters who didn't escape that fate. But to live with that guilt, she would defend herself with determination and pride, with a twinkle in her eye, *sotto voce*, 'but I could *run* and run and run …'

In time, I also found out that the phrase 'curling up like the new moon' referred to, in ancient mythology, the nimble and dainty dancer's feet in highly embroidered slippers that 'curled up like the new moon', a poignant symbol for the nature of the life cycle, of renewal and growth; an insoluble bond between generations, a symbol of continuity, even eternity, binding the old and the new.

I carry Maa Maa's story with me still. It's a reminder of her courage, her bid for freedom and independence. And each new moon is a reminder of her pain as well as her courage, her quiet sense of humour and her strength to let her story live on, like those dreamlike, weightless dancer's feet that dared to tread across millennia.

What a moving story this is, how not being bound by culture gives the freedom to run, to jump, to be free.

The wise child

Another poetic memory of a grandmother is offered by this 'wise child'. There is a role reversal here as she understands her grandmother's conversation with a dead mother.

Sitting on my bed
feet stuck out in front of her,
telephone pressed to her ear
she's silent, far away, listening
to the crackled voice of her own mother …
At last 'Mum?
When are you coming back Mum?'

When she puts the phone down
she doesn't cry. I say
'Let's go to the park.'
We put on her coat and shoes.
Walking along the road she goes slower
and slower and finally stops.

She lies down on the pavement
curled up, eyes closed.

Some people stare
an old lady asks if she's alright?
I nod, sit on the curb beside her
and look up into the plane tree above us.

When I look back her eyes are open –
for a moment as she looks at me,
she is the grandmother, I the child.
She stands up and I brush leaves off her coat.
'Mummy's coming back on Friday.'
She runs ahead to the park, the swings.

The cookie person

Here is a granny fondly remembered as a 'cookie person'.

When Granny died, she left me her electric typewriter. She left my cousin Glenn stocks in the railroad. She left my brother and younger cousin some stocks as well, maybe in the telephone company. My mum told me Granny thought I had Walter (my father) to take care of me—of all the grandchildren, I was the only one whose father hadn't completely disappeared. At any rate, the stocks probably weren't worth much more than the typewriter. My grandfather had been a foreman at the paper mill and Granny had been a wife and home maker. Although they owned their small house and had managed to send their three children to college, they didn't have much else. Still, over time, the stocks would have gone up in value, while the typewriter would be supplanted by a word processor and then by a personal computer. I was the oldest grandchild and the only girl and they all believed I would be a writer. I had won first prize at the local library for a book I wrote when I was twelve and that was my dream.

When I was little my grandmother was always my 'cookie person'. I learned this term years later from a therapist who said there is always someone in your life you remember as being on your side. Literally, there were always homemade cookies at Granny's house. Figuratively she always took my side. When I was less than three, I was very talkative. 'Well, she's not autistic,' my aunt joked, 'she is too artistic!' My grandmother defended me.

We visited Granny and Grandad several times a year, usually for holidays. On the way, my mum would sing 'Over the river and through the woods, to grandmother's house we go'. [*Is there a possible link to Red Riding Hood here?*] It was about a forty-minute drive but when I was little it seemed like an adventure, and the small river where the paper mill was and the small woods along the road made me believe that song had been written for my family.

On the front porch there were ironwork posts that I could climb and in the backyard there were apple trees. In the house there was a little wooden cabinet whose door opened sideways. Inside were board games, cards, and puzzles. I would open that cabinet and find something to play with. One of my favourites was putting wooden pegs into wooden cacti as if they were prickly pears. Granny had a pantry with all kinds of canned goods and preserves and different kinds of cereal, and there was an attic with mysterious memories, including a doll called Pitiful Pearl that had belonged to my mum when she was a little girl.

Usually I went to my grandparents' house with my mum, but when I was five and a half I went to stay two or three nights with them on my own while my brother was being born in the hospital. In order to prepare me for being a big sister, I was given a 'newborn' Thumbelina doll. She wasn't real newborn size, but much smaller. She had a motor inside and a string which made her move her arms and legs like a baby.

I stayed with my grandparents one other time when I was twelve or so. It must have been unexpected as I didn't have proper clothes for church on Sunday. Granny and Grandad took me shopping and I chose a brown paisley dress with lace and ribbons. It was special being bought a new dress just for one occasion.

When I was in high school I took a class in oral history. One of our assignments was to interview our grandparents about their youth. Granny and Grandad were very happy to talk to me. My school was downtown in the city where we lived and they had grown up in that same city. They told me they used to roller-skate all the way from where they lived to the main train station downtown. That was a five-mile roller-skate on a road that was now four lanes and full of cars. When they were teenagers they used to get up early and play tennis before going to school. My grandmother tied a string around her big toe and hung it out her window. In the morning my grandfather tugged on the string, she got up and went quietly downstairs and they walked together to the courts. Then they told me that they wanted to get married and they decided to elope, using the same method! They were barely eighteen.

We went to visit them for Easter when I was fifteen. My mum and my aunt were both in a flurry as my grandmother was showing them something private. They included me as one of the women now and I was invited to see as well. We went to Granny's room and she was rearranging her blouse. She was inserting something into one side of her bra and then asking my mum and my aunt what they thought. How did it look? I didn't fully understand that my grandmother had had a mastectomy.

The next time I remember visiting Granny, she was in her bedroom, in bed. She wasn't getting out of bed. On the radio John Lennon's song *Imagine* was playing. I had recently learned about that song and shared all of the idealism it embodied. I told Granny what the words were. She said, 'I don't understand why those musicians have so much money but there are still so many poor people in the world.' Then she went on to say, 'I don't understand why the people in India are starving but they let cows roam in the street.' I noticed a pin on her dresser that said 'United Daughters of the Confederacy'. I didn't understand that, so I guess we were even.

Granny and Grandad had planned to travel the United States in an auto caravan when Grandad retired. That was their dream. He retired when he was sixty-five, after over forty years of work. Granny was diagnosed with breast cancer the same year and they never got to do their trip. She died two years later, just a little after their fiftieth wedding anniversary. But even though this was when she died, they had fifty good years to remember, years filled largely with love and fellowship.

Special shared moments

Let's move on to the Czech Republic for another memory filled with love.

I spent a lot of time with my grandma when I was younger. She used to take me and collect me from school and take me to swimming classes, then back to her house for my snack and a chat.

Sometimes I would stay over for a sleepover. Her house felt, and still does feel, like a second home. The smells evoke memories of special moments shared. We would bake, something I never did with my parents. We would eat at the table, again not something we did often at my parents' (not that it was an issue but it did make it a novelty). I remember being amazed by the light that came on every time I opened the door to the cupboard under her stairs. We didn't have a cupboard like that in my parents' house. I remember learning about Jewish food, celebrations, and stories. I remember the smell of three tiny bottles of hand lotion in her bathroom decorated with floral labels. They were like mystical potions, a sort of magic. I would watch the frogs swimming in the pond in her garden and pick fruit off the bushes she had grown. I remember a Perspex cube that was filled with photos of my parents and our alsatian Jack and me as a baby. It wound up and played a beautiful song. The memory of that song is tinged with both love and some sadness and I have a vague recollection that the cube was kept on reserve for when I was missing my parents. I remember it being a comfort.

When my grandma got a stair lift, I would spend ages riding it upstairs, downstairs, upstairs, downstairs, it never got boring. The balance of my grandma's space being both such a familiar and comforting place to be whilst also having the novelty of not being the space where I lived full-time was a magical cocktail. Spending time with her has always provided that same magic, no matter the setting. I have always felt lucky to have what I consider to be a third parent. A third loving adult to bring a third perspective into all of our conversations and shared moments.

I do remember her getting annoyed with me from time to time. A repeat offence of mine involved her rug. There was a corner of the rug that landed by her sofa which, as a fidget, I used to play with, using my toes, bending it back and forth as I sat there. She would get very annoyed with me doing it and I never really understood why it was a problem. Of course, I appreciate her frustration now at looking down at an increasingly dog-eared rug! That isn't a negative memory, more of a curious one for me. I never understood why she cared about it so much.

From a very young age my grandma's perspective was often the psychological. She never patronised me. I remember if I had fallen out with a friend, and I seem to remember this being an almost daily occurrence with one kid at school in particular, she would listen and empathise in the way any child needs, but would then steadily move on to ask me questions that made me feel grown up and special and as if I had a unique take on the day's events that would, through our detective work, crack the code of what it had all 'meant'. Her questions, although straightforward, would force us to meander around the events of the day and eventually, together, we would explore not just how I but how others may have been feeling. How the other child might be feeling right now talking to their own adult about the day. Sometimes the questioning would feel frustrating, when in that moment all you want from your adult is blind agreement about your outrage. But by the time we'd driven home (to her house) and I'd started to eat my snack of frankfurters, or sliced red pepper, or Dairylea triangles, the anger and upset of the day's drama had been replaced by calm reflection and sometimes even empathy. Feelings I couldn't yet name, but knew were a special result of our chat. I knew that other children at school weren't so lucky. They didn't know what my grandma and I knew. They didn't think how we thought. I knew they weren't detectives like we were.

Can scary granny change?

And now for something which illustrates how things can morph over time: a scared child recalls a scary granny, with 'cold bony hands, long fingers', almost a scary skeleton. But as the child grows, becomes an adolescent and then an adult, she sees her granny in a different, more benign light.

My granny was someone I felt a bit scared of. Mind you, I was scared of most things back then in the 1950s. She was a small woman and I remember the smell of face powder and her cold, bony hands with long fingers. My dread was of the front door greeting when we visited, the appalling realisation that I was expected to kiss her. It was like a wall beyond which all was forced and proper and neat and tidy and I couldn't breathe, let alone relax and enjoy myself. There was a great emphasis on cleanliness of hands and feet, and she would immediately fuss around us, taking our coats and shoes, wiping our hands, and inviting my brother and me into the sitting room to amuse ourselves making houses of cards while she would talk to my parents in the kitchen about grown-up things. I remember my breathing changing and my tummy jumping all the while, doing what we should do as good children under constraint. On our journey home in the car we would start to relax, told that we had been good, giggling on the back seat with my brother, breath freeing itself a bit.

This was post-war Britain. My granny had lived through their house being damaged by aircraft guns, growing vegetables as a matter of course, her husband being away with war business, having three boys to look after. Reading her diaries now, it is fascinating to see her careful accounts of money spent, twice-weekly visits to the cinema, and morning coffee meetings with other women folk, alongside German air raids on the seaside town.

As I grew up in London, Granny would take my brother and me out on a bus to Bentalls for a milkshake or up to the Festival Hall for a concert. I remember being told not to touch the escalator hand rail for fear of germs, and horror of horror I remember her finger going up my nostril to check it was clean whilst in public on a bus journey. She cut our finger nails so short that they would hurt and I remember my mother being upset at the implied criticism of her care of us. Then of all surreal injunctions told to young children, she warned us to beware of the 'night dogs'. [*Dogs may howl at night, and some may take this as a portent of death. The dogs, of course, are the after-runners of wolves …*]

However, as I grew up and became a teenager, I found her to be a deeper and kinder person than I had appreciated in my early years and I developed a personal relationship that became important to my life. In talking about her life before she married, I discovered that she had worked as a dancer and cabaret artiste in a travelling entertainment troupe. She dug out old photos and press cuttings for me to see. She told me how she wove elastic into the women's vests for support because bras attached in corsetry weren't suitable for dancing in those days. I asked her to teach me ballet in her tiny kitchen, we would have lunches together and I would leave feeling nourished in body and mind. I looked forward to seeing her now. We shared another life beyond uptight fear of germs, survival of war, and the night dogs. She made me indulgent chocolate cakes to take back to miserable boarding school, wrote me letters with a five pound note in them, and I would write back to her with a feeling that I could be my authentic self. When I began to lead an unconventional life as an adult, we still wrote and I didn't feel judged. When I had a baby without being married, she loved him and loved me. The generational remove from my parents proved a valuable support for me when in reality I was going through a time of turmoil. Looking back now I can see that she was more important to me than I gave her credit for at the time.

So, as Melanie Klein showed in her clinical work, memories and indeed recall of experiences can change over time, so that parents previously thought to be uncaring and cut off can be reinstated in the ego as more positive influences or, as we would say in psychoanalytic speak, 'positive objects'. This granny turned from being a frightening object to one more benign, listening in an empathic and non-judgemental way to the unfolding life of her little grandchild and encouraging the growth of empathy in the little girl herself, growing up to be an independent woman.

Auntie Annie fills the void

In this story, where grandparents are lost early in life, someone else steps in.

My grandmothers both died when I was two years old. I know I had a relationship with them both as I can see it in photographs, and now that I have my own grandchildren I know how deeply connected I feel to them and that this depth of connection exists before they are two years old. And yet I only have photographs and things that my parents have told me about them. I have no memories. I didn't often feel that they were missing from my life, but I vividly remember feeling jealous of my best friend Fiona's hand-knitted socks, which her grandma had knitted for her. They represented something I knew I didn't have.

Not long after that my dad's godmother, who we called Auntie Annie, started to look after me and my sister every Wednesday after school and in school holidays because Mum had a part-time job. I loved the time spent with Auntie Annie and the stories she told me of her early life, and of my dad when he was little, and of my paternal grandmother Minnie, who had been Annie's best friend. Auntie Annie filled a gap I hadn't realised was there and she became our surrogate grandmother. I loved how different she was from my parents' generation. I liked that she was frugal even though it meant when she made a cake there was very little left in the bowl for me to lick. I loved that she was there when my grandparents first went on a date, as Minnie wanted her support, even though she was hidden watching from afar. She told me that my grandmother was beautiful and that she loved to dance, and that was how she met my grandad, who was a pianist in a dance band.

Auntie Annie was a natural storyteller and the stories of her own family when she was small had me spellbound. She made our cups of tea in bone china cups with saucers and read my tea leaves after every cup. She had a little box on the window sill full of tiny scrolls of paper. I used to ask to pick one every time I went to see her and each one was a verse from the Bible. She was widowed in her early fifties and I never met Arthur Dawtrey, her husband and father of her two boys, but she said she loved him alone and never looked at another man after he died. She loved fiercely, and she loved my dad the same way, and in turn I also felt her love. All her family lived to a good age (those that survived childhood) and Annie was in her late eighties when she died. I have so many memories and stories of her, and what this experience says to me is that you don't have to be a blood relative to be grandmother to a child.

Non-repeating patterns?

Let's look at patterns that are not necessarily repeated.

My relationship with both my grandmothers was very different. I don't remember them being at all affectionate and certainly not fun. They were born during the reign of Queen Victoria and were from the generation where children were seen and not heard.

There was certainly no talking at the table and it was pretty much speak when you are spoken to.

My mum brought me up as a single parent from the age of five until I was seventeen, when she remarried. I was a horrible child and teenager and treated my mum very badly. For years I wanted to go and live with my dad as I thought the grass would be greener. It was not until I was married with my own children that I realised just how awful I had been and I really don't know how I would have coped if my boys treated me the same way. This I have regretted all my adult life.

My relationship with my grandmothers and my mother made me so determined to do better. Hopefully I have.

Idealisation: its importance in every life

Below we have writ large the importance of idealisation. To each grandma, each child is precious and unique and special, a recipient of 'grand-maternal preoccupation' to requote Winnicott rather differently. The grandmas in this story were happily out and about in the workforce when their first grandchild arrived. So no rocking chairs for them.

It pleases me hugely that, during my lifetime, I had the tremendous privilege of enjoying some forty-five years of regular contact with my paternal grandmother, Daphne, and some fifty years of regular contact with my maternal grandmother, Margaret—two extraordinarily loving women. I cannot imagine what my life would feel like had I not had the benefit of so much attention and care and interest and engagement from these two spectacular people.

In retrospect, I believe that each of these relatives demonstrated a real sense of what we might call (drawing upon the work of Winnicott, 1956) 'primary *grand*maternal preoccupation'. Both Daphne and Margaret made all of their grandchildren feel special—rather like little superstars! For instance, my grandmother Margaret often told me, You are so handsome. You look just like Cary Grant. Needless to say, I don't resemble Cary Grant in any way. I have more ordinary and less memorable looks. Ah well. But from Grandma Margaret's perspective, one could tell that she really fell in love with me from my babyhood and regarded me as someone of value. In doing so, she provided much comfort and safety and generosity of spirit.

Nowadays, many women and men don't become parents until they reach their late thirties or early forties. Consequently, large numbers of new, contemporary grandparents will already have reached sixty or seventy or eighty years of age and therefore might be rather old and even infirm and could, perhaps, struggle to devote themselves energetically to the grandchildren. Daphne and Margaret, by contrast, became grandparents at a very young age and I suspect that I simply could not have had such rich and frequent contact with these two women if they had not given birth to their own children—my mother and my father—while still quite young themselves.

Daphne first became a mother at the age of twenty-two and Margaret did so at the age of twenty-one. My own mother then gave birth to me at the age of twenty-one. Therefore, I had a rather special experience of revelling in much affection from an energetic *forty-three-year-old* paternal grandmother and a *forty-two-year-old* maternal grandmother. Thus, I knew these women throughout their forties, fifties, sixties, seventies, and into their eighties. I appreciate that not many people nowadays will have had the honour and privilege of such a great treat. Thus, I do believe that the youthfulness and longevity of my grandmothers will have made a huge contribution to their capacity to be healthy, available, and alert, and to protect me and my siblings from the inevitability of ageing, illness, and death for as long as possible.

In retrospect, I suppose that my grandmothers may have idealised me and my siblings. But in doing so, they made us all feel truly loved, and that emotionality facilitated our sense of confidence and our belief that we might, in fact, deserve a place in the world. I owe Daphne and Margaret a lifetime of unparalleled gratitude.

Three wise monkeys

This chapter ends with the reminiscences of someone who went on to become a child and adolescent psychotherapist—a sort of grandma in her own right. And the three wise monkeys came to have a different significance.

The first thing that came to mind when I thought about grand-mothers was a small brass ornament of three monkeys known as the three wise monkeys: see no evil, hear no evil, and speak no evil. We visited my paternal grandparents every Sunday afternoon and it was a soulless place, devoid of toys. They weren't poor and the house was spacious and well decorated, but the only playthings on offer were the monkeys, a brass and leather bellows, which one was only allowed one go of, and the special treat of the light being put on in the tropical fish tank for five minutes before it was cast into darkness again. Things improved dramatically when one or both of dad's sisters arrived and the house was filled with chatter and camaraderie. My only memory of my paternal grandmother was that she was straight-backed and straightlaced.

I never met my maternal grandparents as they had both died before I was born, but, when I thought about it, my mother formed relationships with women who took on that role and supported her as a mother. The first was Elsie, the next-door neighbour when the eldest three of us were small, and the second was Mrs Turton, after our younger two siblings were born. I remember these women as warm and nurturing and they offset my mother's tendencies towards depression, anxiety, and hypochondriasis.

I began working with children and families in my early twenties and was surprised when parents and grandparents treated me as though I had the knowledge and expertise to help them. I felt a long way from that and somewhat of a charlatan. I learned over time that the role involved the antithesis of the three wise monkeys. Far from turning a blind eye, one was required to see and hear the pain, the hatred, the despair, and, at times, cruelty, and to think very hard about what to say and when to say it. I was to learn that it was easy to work with a child or young person on their own, but this was at the risk of becoming a competitor with the parents: an alternative idealised figure who did little to mitigate the fractures in their daily lives. Taking something of a grandparental position where one worked at developing empathy and compassion for the parents and the children was painful and hard, but where successful reaped the reward of hope for their future relationships.

So as we can see from the memories and fond reminiscences in this chapter, good early relationships with grandmothers can be formative. This last contributor makes a crucial point about not being in competition with the parents but working alongside in an empathic way, perhaps not saying much at all but allowing the parents to come to their own (maybe different) conclusions. It is crucial not to come from some sort of 'superior' position (which could be termed narcissistic) but to be alongside, in mutual listening and reflecting. This is how the best work is done, humanly as well as psychoanalytically.

CHAPTER 8

And what can we conclude, Miss Marple?

In which we sum up what we may have learned along the way

Journey's end. Have we arrived at the same old place or somewhere new? The similarities between criminal detection stories and life are myriad: you can read (or choose not to read) the signs, follow up on clues, deconstruct one narrative and replace it with another. But perhaps there is also a flawed premise in the overall narrative here: the idea that we live in a logical universe and every sign is a route to a solution. Not so. If we think of the art of 'being a Grandmother' as performance art, can what starts as a sort of fetishised view become a whole field? Writing this book has come out of the writing of it in itself, with the help of so many others, a kind of conversation where there are no masters (or mistresses), only other thinkers to draw some of the many conclusions we might draw, in the business of being alive. This is also true of the best kind of psychotherapeutic endeavour, where no one person imposes a particular point of view. As the last contributor in the previous chapter said:

> I was to learn that it was easy to work with a child or young person on their own, but this was at the risk of becoming a competitor with the parents: an alternative idealised figure who did little to mitigate the fractures in their daily lives. Taking something of a grandparental position where one worked at developing empathy and compassion for the parents and the children was

painful and hard, but where successful reaped the reward of
hope for their future relationships.

In 'the pursuit of truth', we aim to recreate the flavour of lived experience.
We helpfully allow people to come to their own conclusions, their
own independent reality, but this is a vulnerable state: as Freud said,
'Recovery leads to danger'.

The novelist Agatha Christie's popular female sleuth Miss Marple
solves crimes that have the police puzzled, and I'm asking her help here
in unravelling all the complications which lie under the 'grandmother'
meme or myth. The author herself said the inspiration for the character
of Miss Marple came from a number of sources, and in 2008 some
previously undiscovered tapes revealed that Miss Marple had been based
on Christie's own grandmother. Previously Christie had been reported
to have said that Miss Marple would have been rather like some of her
step-grandmother's Ealing friends. Miss Marple never married and had
no close living relatives. Though she may seem frail, her mind is forever
sharp and she frequently solves the mystery, in large part by simply paying
close attention to the evidence. Which I hope we have done here.

One of the best-known Miss Marples was the actor Margaret
Rutherford, who herself had a difficult life. An only child born in
1892 in London, Margaret's uncle Sir John Benn was a British politician
and her first cousin once removed was Labour politician Tony Benn.
Margaret's father had murdered his own father in a fit of deep depression
for which he was later hospitalised, so hoping to start a new life far from the
scene of their troubles, the Rutherfords emigrated to India. But Margaret
was returned to London when she was three years old to live with her aunt
after her pregnant mother committed suicide. What almost unimaginable
pain, and guilt too, there must have been for the little girl. Young Margaret
had been told that her father died of a broken heart soon after, so at the
age of twelve she was shocked to learn that her father had actually been
readmitted to Broadmoor Hospital in 1903, where he remained in care
until his death in 1921. Her parents' mental afflictions led Margaret to fear
that she might succumb to similar maladies and these fears haunted her
for the rest of her life. She suffered intermittent bouts of depression and
anxiety. Are we surprised? She had no children, thus no grandchildren,
but is certainly a woman to be celebrated nonetheless.

Granny in the twenty-first century

How can the intergenerational story help or hinder what happens in the twenty-first century to grannies? We have to factor in postnatal depression, even psychosis, and the mother-in-law meme here. One of the sad outcomes of postnatal depression can be aggression against parents, or parents-in-law. There can be a battle for power as a wife over the son of another woman, and no signs of forgiveness (an all-too-common scenario explored in Chapter 6). Although the mother-in-law 'joke' is mainly told by men, the mother-in-law can be a potent threat to a wife who feels threatened internally herself, inferior or not good enough, and who wants to be in sole possession of her husband beyond any idea of sharing with his mother, even though she is now a mother herself. These two often very different women are indeed 'reluctantly related' by marriage, and different views of what constitutes 'normal' can remain a potent issue.

There may of course have been a very close bond between mother and son which hasn't resulted in any or enough separation, but there may also be difficulties with a daughter-in-law's own mother that get displaced onto her in-law. Again, it requires careful, patient work to unravel what may be the real difficulty at the heart of each particular situation. This has a great deal in common with critical theory, which is an approach to social philosophy (and psychoanalysis) that focuses on reflective assessment and observation of society and culture to reveal and challenge existing 'norms'. What I have argued here is that social attitudes may stem from current social structures and cultural assumptions as well as from the internal worlds of individuals, though these still have their place of course. If we think that the way we think now is the principal obstacle to human liberation, let's free ourselves from 'the norm' and find a more nuanced approach.

Perhaps what we can say with some certainty is that our past experiences colour everything, but do not necessarily define the future. As we saw in the last chapter, poor maternal relationships can motivate new mothers to 'do better'—or vice versa. As quantum theory theorist David Mermin says, 'You just have to accept that all knowledge begins with individual personal experience.' Each of us builds a set of beliefs about the world, based on our interactions with it. The 'big reality' in which we all live emerges from the collisions of our subjective mini-realities. So the idea of a single objective reality is an illusion. A group of quantum mechanics theorists have interpreted the world as 'Qbism' (pronounced Cubism, like the art movement). They suggest that each of us constructs a set of beliefs about the world, based on our interactions with it. What we suggest here is that the future may be just the past waiting to happen again, unless we intervene. The events of the past can have a profound effect on how we see our lives now and what we choose to believe about our world, as I have indicated in this book. Will you feel a bit different after you've finished the book? Our past experiences can influence our emotional reactions and responses to present events. Each of us reacts to stimuli based on what we have learned in life. There is no right or wrong to it, it is simply the result of past experience. This is repeated as it is crucial and we need to think about it more than once, we need to think about it in order to digest it, many times. We are all entangled in the past, the vagaries of the present and the unknowable future. We may be more alive to the contradictions within the self as we reflect on our own actions and the actions of others: we move inwards to move onwards. Inner-standing as well as under-standing moves us on.

Between stimulus and instant reaction exists a fleeting moment of thought, as I have previously said. Often, that thought is based on something that has happened to you in the past. When presented with a similar situation later on, your natural impulse is unconsciously to regard it in a similar light. For example, if you survived a traumatic car accident as a youngster, the first thing you might feel upon seeing even a minor collision may be intense panic. If you still have unpleasant associations with death from a past experience, you may find yourself unable to think about death as a gentle release or the next step towards a new kind of existence. You can, however, minimise the intensity of your reactions by identifying the momentary thought that inspires your reaction. Then, next time, replace that thought with a more positive one. So easy to say, obvious even, but so hard to do. Much depends on our internal strategies based on our first interactions in childhood. It's vital to realise that emotions are our regular guests: welcoming them and seeing what they bring to the table is an excellent first step.

The Oedipus story is one of our most compelling myths. It was Freud who discovered that it was universally relevant to family life. Mother, father, and child, the essential triangle. Anyone who needs a reminder of how that works and the subtle geometry it involves could read the Irish writer Frank O'Connor's short story 'My Oedipus Complex', in which one small boy struggles to find a place in the family alongside his mother and his father and the new baby brother. (Who's been sleeping in *my* bed?)

There can be lies which divide us fatally from aspects of ourselves, multifaceted beings as we all are, and that of course includes psychotherapists, who may wish to be viewed as omniscient but are prey like everyone else to the patchwork of ideas and feelings inside. To maintain a lie we have to build a scaffold round it, to separate it off from doubts and questions, different points of view. This leads to insistent defensiveness, as though by such defensiveness the other side of the lie becomes unreachable and inaccessible. Complexity and understanding can be suppressed. It happens to us all when we're cornered, with our backs to the wall. Outrage at someone else's point of view is a way of strengthening our own position.

But understanding the 'why' does not make the 'now' any more manageable or digestible. Sometimes a clear boundary needs to be drawn and those with so-called 'failed' relationships as grandmothers might do better to turn to better relationships, of which there are always some, rather than drown in an ocean of possibilities that never happened.

Going back to the Introduction, are therapy and therapeutic understanding any good at unravelling all this, separating the Good, the Bad, and the Ugly? Impulsive action gets rid of feeling but does it help? If—and it's a big if—we can learn to tolerate uncertainty and wait if need be, that's a huge start. A crucial question is, does myth begin with a lie or a deception? What are the takeaways here, if any? There are some paradoxes inherent in the grandmother meme: while 'off her rocker' was coined in the eighteenth century to denote being mad, Grandma is certainly off her rocker now in a literal way. In order to remain young, or young enough, she may still work into her seventies and eighties, even though, since women are having children later, Granny may be quite a bit older than her predecessors and, as I have said, may find the tasks she is asked to do quite exhausting.

The nineteenth-century psychologist and philosopher William James had quite a good view on this. He thought we were all 'a bundle of habits'. He defined the concept of neuroplasticity before it was generally accepted as a concept, and in this book I have attempted to explore some of our habitual ideas in order to reset our current patterns of thought.

James makes a case for consistency of effort, offering one final vital idea: just as, if we let our emotions evaporate, they get into a habit of evaporating, so there is reason to suppose that if we often flinch from making an effort, before we know it the effort-making capacity will be gone, and if we suffer the wandering of our attention, presently it will wander all the time. Use it or lose it, as the saying goes. Attention and effort are two names for the same psychic fact. But I would like to add that wandering can sometimes produce new ways of thinking. As someone once wrote in a book of mine, 'not all who wander are lost'.

Castles in the air are built, and like sandcastles they may get swept away by the tide of unexpected events like birth and what happens afterwards. In my experience over thirty years, what is always noteworthy is the emotional distance we can all travel from rigidity and fear to acceptance of one another. This involves overcoming our previous defensiveness in order to become freer. We learn to talk, from the deep heart's core, as Yeats said. It's a hard road but worth it.

'Christopher Robin', based on A. A. Milne's son (A. A. Milne spent a lot of his time writing rather than relating to his little boy, so it is said), has a lot of fun with his toys and chief among them is the redoubtable Pooh Bear. For Christopher Robin, life as a small boy is fairly simple. 'It means just going along, listening to all the things you can't hear, and not bothering,' he tells Pooh. But he adds, wistfully, in Milne's last book, that he can't do Nothing any more. The time has come. 'They' won't let you do Nothing any more. He makes Pooh promise never to forget him, even when they grow old. Pooh promises. This marks the end of Christopher Robin's enchanted childhood. But before this sad goodbye, when the Heffalump doesn't heffalump along, Piglet rushes to get Christopher Robin to help. Is a Granny rather like a Heffalump according to where you stand? The little boy rescues Pooh from the Very Deep Pit and he laughs and laughs. This book is not about judging 'right' and 'wrong', but about trying to find meaning as we all try to do in the vagaries of life as it happens. We may have gone down some rabbit holes but we've found a warren underneath there, full of new meanings and new ideas. Some of them may have previously been unconscious, or as an adolescent I saw once said with a wry smile, 'Well, not consciously, but I know it somewhere.' While you may still subscribe to the myth of the grandmother meme, she may have 'left the building' in her previous form. There has been no attempt to prove anything here, but improving ideas about these issues hopefully has been an outcome.

Perhaps it's not unfitting to end with a word from a poem by the legendary thirteenth-century Sufi Persian poet Rumi, which sums up the conflicts and different views inherent in this as in any theme, no matter what time and place we are in, imperfect human beings as we all are. Rumi talked about a field beyond the rigid ideas of who is 'wrong' and who is 'right'. He suggested we meet there, in an open field, without judgement, and I hope we have done that.

Bibliography

Ahlberg, J. & Ahlberg, A. (1999). *The Jolly Postman*. London: Puffin.

Australian Human Rights Commission (1997). Bringing them home. https://humanrights.gov.au/our-work/bringing-them-home-report-1997 (last accessed 24 August 2023).

Bardon, G. & Bardon, J. (2004). *Papunya: A Place Made After the Story*. Melbourne: Miegunyah Press.

Barrow, C. (1998). *Family in the Caribbean: Themes and Perspectives*. New Jersey: Markus Wiener Pub Inc.

Bettelheim, B. (1991). *The of Enchantment*. London: Penguin.

Bion, W. R. (1962). *Learning from Experience*. London: Karnac.

Bion, W. R. (1991). *A Memoir of the Future*. London: Karnac.

Brann, D. (2016). *Reluctantly Related: Secrets to Getting Along with Your Mother-in-Law or Daughter-in-Law*. Ambergris.

Brann, D. (2016). *Reluctantly Related Revisited: Breaking Free of the Mother-in-Law/Daughter-in-Law Conflict*. Ambergris.

Brodber, E. (2014). *Nothing's Mat*. Kingston: University of West Indies Press.

Connolly, C. (2018). *Intergenerational Transmission, Projective Identification, and Parent-Work: A Theoretical and Clinical Study*. Unpublished PhD dissertation.

Dahl, R. (2016). *Revolting Rhymes*. London: Puffin.

Edwards, J. (2012). *Pieces of Molly*. London: Karnac.

Edwards, J. (2017). *Love the Wild Swan: The Selected Works of Judith Edwards*. Abingdon, UK: Routledge.

Fraiberg, S., Adelson, E., & Shapiro, V. (1974). Ghosts in the nursery: A psychoanalytic approach to the problems of impaired. *Journal of American Academy of Child Psychiatry*, 14(3): 387–421.

Freud, S. (1900a). *The Interpretation of Dreams. S. E., 4*: ix–627. London: Hogarth.

Freud, S. (1915d). Repression. *S. E., 14*: 141–158. London: Hogarth.

Freud, S. (1919h). The 'uncanny'. *S. E., 17*: 217–256. London: Hogarth.

Freud, S. (1937c). Analysis terminable and interminable. *S. E., 23*: 209–254. London: Hogarth.

Gerard, J. M., Landry-Meyer, L., & Roe, J. G. (2006). Grandparents raising grandchildren: The role of social support in coping with caregiving challenges. *The International Journal of Aging and Human Development, 62*(4): 359–383. https://doi.org/10.2190/3796-DMB2-546Q-Y4AQ

Haven, C. L. (2018). *Evolution of Desire: A Life of René Girard*. Michigan: Michigan State University Press.

Henry, R. M. (2020). Borderland territory in developmental creativity. In: J. Edwards (Ed.), *Psychoanalysis and Other Matters. Where Are We Now?* Abingdon, UK: Routledge.

Kellermann, N. P. (2001). Transmission of Holocaust trauma—an integrative view. *Psychiatry Interpersonal & Biological Processes, 64*(3): 256–267.

Kessler, D. (2019). *Finding Meaning: The Sixth Stage of Grief*. New York City: Scribner.

Klein, M. (1988). *Envy and Gratitude and Other Works 1946–63*. London: Hogarth Press.

Kusano, E., Ono, M., & Hayakawa, K. (2010). Influence of support by elderly persons on Japanese mothers' child care-related stress. *Nursing and Health Sciences, 12*(2): 182–190. https://doi.org/10.1111/j.1442-2018.2010.00516.x

Larkin, P. (1988). *Collected Poems*. London: Faber.

Mantel, H. (2009). *Wolf Hall*. London: Fourth Estate (p. 529).

Marhankova, J. H. (2015). The role of grandmother in Czech families today. *Czech Sociological Review, 51*(5).

McCulloch, S. & McCulloch Childs, E. (2001). *Contemporary Aboriginal Art: The Complete Guide*. Melbourne: McCulloch & McCulloch.

Mermin, D. (1968). *Space and Time in Special Relativity*. Illinois: Waveland Press.

Parkes, C. M. (2015). *The Price of Love: The Selected Works of Colin Murray Parkes*. Abingdon, UK: Routledge.

Payne, A. M. (2021). *Stolen Motherhood: Aboriginal Mothers and Child Removal in the Stolen Generations Era*. Kentucky: Lexington Books.

Reitzes, D. C. & Mutran, E. J. (1994). Multiple roles and identities: Factors influencing self-esteem among middle-aged working men and women. *Social Psychology Quarterly, 57*(4): 313–325. https://doi.org/10.2307/2787158

Renaud, L. (2018). *Representations of Afro-Caribbean Matrifocality*. PhD dissertation.

Renaud, L. (2020). Beyond the nuclear: The Caribbean family. *History Workshop*, https://www.historyworkshop.org.uk/family-childhood/beyond-the-nuclear-the-caribbean-family/ (last accessed 4 October 2023).

Rovelli, C. (2019). *The Order of Time*. London: Penguin.

Sandel, T. L., Cho, G. E., Miller, P. J., & Wang, S.-H. (2006). What it means to be a grandmother: A cross-cultural study of Taiwanese and Euro-American grandmothers' beliefs. *Journal of Family Communication, 6*(4): 255–278. https://doi.org/10.1207/s15327698jfc0604_2

Setiawan, E. (2009). *Of Bees and Mists*. London: Simon & Schuster.

Shakespeare's Sonnets (1609). London: Thomas Thorpe.

Simpson, J. (2014). Reviving indigenous languages—not as easy as it seems. https://theconversation.com/reviving-indigenous-languages-not-as-easy-as-it-seems-68977 (last accessed 24 August 2023).

Slutzker, J. (2011). Engaging grandmothers: Israeli and Palestinian women share their stories. *Palestine-Israel Journal of Politics, Economics and Culture, Women and Power, 17*(3). https://pij.org/articles/1379/engaging-grandmothers-israeli-and-palestinian-women-sharetheir-stories (last accessed 15 August 2023).

Smith, R. T. (1996). *The Matrifocal Family: Power, Pluralism and Politics.* New York and Abingdon, UK: Routledge.

Wilson, A. N. (2014). *Victoria: A Life.* London: Atlantic Books.

Winnicott, D. W. (1956). Primary maternal preoccupation. In: L. Caldwell & H. T. Robinson (Eds.), *The Collected Works of D. W. Winnicott: Volume 5, 1955–1959.* New York: Oxford University Press, 2016.

Index